The God of Our Journey

To

Victor

With
love

From Ivy

The Spastics Society

The God of Our Journey

Michael Walker

Marshall Pickering

Marshall Morgan and Scott
Marshall Pickering
34–42 Cleveland Street, London, W1P 5FB. U.K.

First published in 1989 by Marshall Morgan and Scott Publications Ltd
Part of the Marshall Pickering Holdings Group

British Library Cataloguing in Publication Data
Walker, Michael, *1932–*
    God of our journey
    1. Christian life – Personal observations
    I. Title
    248.4 ISBN 0–551–01833–X

Text Set in Linotron Baskerville by Input Typesetting Ltd., London
Printed in Great Britain by Cox and Wyman, Reading.

Contents

Introduction

Writing in the dark years of the Second World War, the American theologian John A. Mackay said that there were two perspectives from which to look at Christian theology. They were the perspectives of the balcony and road.

The first image he took from Spain, where the balcony obtrudes from the front of the house, looking down on the road. It provides a vantage point from which the spectator can see the passing traffic and people going about their errands or making their journeys. It is the perspective of the spectator, of someone who is stationary, travelling nowhere.

The road is the place of journeying. Here, one is affected by the movements of other people. One is no longer above what is happening, but part of it. Nor does one stand still. The road has an end and it has a beginning. At any point along the road, we can recount the story of our journey thus far and share the hopes we have of the journey still to be covered and the destination to be reached.

Theology, claimed Mackay, is to be worked through on the road. It is not a spectator activity. The theologian does not sit at a vantage point above the rest of the world. If he is to be a theologian, then he must be where others are and reflect on his own journey. As the theologians of the Orthodox church have always affirmed, true theology always ends in prayer. It has to do with our own Christian pilgrimage and the growth of our own spiritual life.

A theology that is written in abstraction from its author's pilgrimage or the bustling flow of human life by which he is surrounded is one that has detached itself from the only environment within which it has meaning. Speculating on how many angels can stand on the head of a pin is relevant only when the last place left on earth for anyone to stand is the pin's head and we wonder how much space there is to share.

The journey, which a Christian calls pilgrimage and to which he or she is committed throughout the whole of life, is one in which we increase in our understanding of God. No matter how overwhelming the experience with which we begin, how dramatic our conversion, how breathtaking our vision of God and what he has done for us, it is but a beginning. Life itself will face us with experiences and demands that will be constantly requiring us to sort out in our minds how what we believe relates to what is happening to us and around us.

In the pages that follow, I reflect on what God means to me where I am now. It is a reflection that is unashamedly theological. This is not because I earn my living as a professional theologian. It is because I have always wanted to find words for the God who is beyond words, who strives to reveal himself in the world and in the unfolding of our pilgrimage.

Closely allied with my conviction that Christian pilgrimage is about growing in our knowledge and love of God is another. To grow in Christ is to grow as a human being. At the core of the Christian faith is the shattering belief that God revealed himself most fully in the fully human life of Jesus of Nazareth. This is the glory of the Christian faith. There is no place on earth and no experience from which we cannot turn to Christ and find him there, one with us, sharing it with us as Son of Man and Son of God.

It is a perspective that is not universally self-evident. There has always been a dimension to Christianity that has treated the human with contempt and sought knowledge of God by rejecting the world. I am not referring to the monastic Christian tradition which I respect deeply and to which I owe more than I can say; rather, to a tendency on the part of Christians to create Christian enclaves, all too subject to what is worldly in the worst sense and valuing the super-human a great deal more than the human.

I do not believe that we can escape the implications of the flesh and blood that Christ became in order to reveal the one, eternal Father; or the flesh and blood which, transformed and set free from the power of death, he brought with him from the tomb on the morning of the resurrection; or the flesh and blood which are given to us in the holy Eucharist. All of them compel us to look to the human for our knowledge of God, and to affirm the glorious possibilities for our human life in Jesus Christ. They point to the destination of our humanity and teach us, here and now, to value the material and the substantial as the means by which God makes himself known and gives himself to us.

Chapter One

The God of Our Journey

Ever since Jesus called his first disciples to follow him, the theme of journey has remained central to the Christian life. It is a theme that has its roots within the Judaism from which Jesus himself came. Abraham, like James, John Peter, Matthew and the other apostles, left the only life he knew to embark on one that had faith as its only guide. The early Christians, like the Jews leaving Egypt on Passover night, set out on a journey to a promised land; the spread of whose scenery could be visualised only in the imagination. For Christians and Jews alike, the journey follows a route traced by faith and heads for a destination known only in hope.

There are two aspects of the journey. There is the journey that can be plotted across the physical landscape of time and place. Its route lies through the family from which we come, the progress of the career we choose, the places where we live, the churches to which we belong and, most importantly, the people who travel with us.

There is another journey, the inner journey that runs along the tracks of mind, heart, will, memory and imagination. It lies through that inner country that people of another generation called the soul. It lies beyond the sight of most and even those who are closest to us can follow it only in part. It is a journey towards maturity which, for Christians, is that stature which, as Paul described it, belongs to nothing less than the fullness of Christ.[1]

1

Our progress towards maturity, Paul again persuades us in the matchless prose of his hymn to love,[2] is one that comes to its completion only in the life to come. In this life, we have 'no continuing city', no permanence, we are always on the way.[3]

The word soul has already slipped into our thinking. We have spoken of outer and inner journeys. We must be cautious. There are not two divorced worlds existing in isolation from one another, nor are there parallel roads down which our lives follow their course. There are warnings enough in what theology and philosophy, as well as the data of our own experience, teach us. Body cannot be sundered from soul, nor outward circumstances from the person who lives through them. It is a lesson that we are reluctant to learn. Even our confident handling of concepts like 'body' and 'soul', the time-honoured abstractions of intellectual debate, can conceal our unwillingness to merge into one the human and the spiritual. In pursuing our spiritual goals, we imagine that the human can be shunted off the track of our central concerns. We divorce the desire to become a better Christian from the need to grow as a human Leing.

All human growth involves the constant inter-action between body and soul, between what we experience in our senses and what we imagine with our minds, between what we believe with our reason and what we experience in our flesh and blood. Similarly, both mind and body play their part in the growth of our faith. For those in the Judaeo-Christian tradition, religion can never be disembodied or teased out from the many inter-mingling strands that form our experience. We cannot 'succeed' as Christians whilst 'failing' as human beings.

The material world, the present home of our souls, is the scene of God's revelation of himself to us. It is here, in the visible and the human that, with the eyes of faith, we learn to recognise him. The human is not a second-rate alternative to the spiritual. In this life, the spiritual has no

other home but the human; it is through our senses that
eternal realities are mediated to us. We *hear* the word of
God, we *see* his glory. John the Apostle spoke of God's
revelation as that which 'we have seen with our own
eyes . . . looked upon . . . felt with our own hands'.[4]

Similarly, it is through human that faith finds its expression. Believers do not inhabit a world different from others.
There is a common reservoir of human experience, from
birth to death, that we all share. Our path to maturity lies
through situations that are replicated time without number
in the lives of those who do not share our faith.

We may yearn for the superhuman in a vain attempt to
distance ourselves from others. If only we can rise above
the human, we believe, then we will, in some way, become
more authentic Christian men and women. We are rooted
in the human, however, and we cannot escape from it
without losing that which is our authentic identity, the
identity of a man or woman made in the image of God.

Similarly, we believe that faith finds its most telling
confirmation in the supernatural. But again, the supernatural is seen as a way of transcending, rather than transfiguring, the limitations of being human. The supernatural
represents the clear vision of God within the world that he
has made, it is not an escape route to another world free
from the constraints of the created order. That goodness
which is the goal of all true maturity is not a state in which
the human has been left behind. It is one in which it is
transformed by the love of God and in which the divine
glory takes a human form.

To try to escape from the human is to retreat from what
God has given us, to choose other battlefields on which to
quit ourselves as Christians. Worst of all, in our flight from
the human, we pass, going in the opposite direction, that
living Word of whom Julian of Norwich said, 'God's Son
fell with Adam, into the valley of the womb of the maiden
who was the fairest daughter of Adam'.[5] The central conviction of the Christian faith is that God has revealed

himself most clearly in his Son who was made man and came incarnate in our flesh and blood.

If the spiritual cannot be separated from the human, neither can we escape the lifelong process that forms our growth to maturity. In spite of the biblical witness, we are not always convinced about the need to keep moving. The journey is always longer than we want it to be. Wishing to free ourselves from the prospect of further pain, we persuade ourselves, too soon, that maturity is already ours. For, undoubtedly, growing to maturity is a painful process. By calling a premature halt to our journey, we hope to be spared further discomfort, to achieve by remaining stationary what others come to only by travelling. This temptation to lay premature claim to a maturity already achieved may be illustrated by three areas of our lives.

For example, we can come to what we believe to be journey's end in the way we view our religious beliefs, trading the dialogue between faith and doubt for dogmatisms that leave no room for doubt. Not that we should become professional doubters, holding every truth at arm's length as if nothing could be embraced close to the heart. There are truths that grow in their brightness as the journey progresses. Time teaches us that even if resurrection as an experience may be at times overwhelmed by the darkness, nevertheless as truth believed it does not desert us. The affirmation that Christ is risen becomes as basic to our perception of the world as the assurance that the sun will rise tomorrow. Such assurance, however, is not to be confused with a dogmatism that refuses to acknowledge the existence of questions to which there are no answers. To say, 'Christ is risen' is not the same as reciting a multitude of dogmatic words like an incantation designed to protect us from what is unnerving and disturbing. Our beliefs only grow in conviction as they become battle-scarred. Even when we cannot share the agnostic's uncertainty we can retain some sympathy for his or her predicament and some understanding of why she or he continues to ask questions.

Then again, we may stop growing in our human relationships. The world of our infancy is a world dominated by our own needs. Gradually we become aware of the existence of mother and father, figures upon whom we are dependent but who also represent the existence of a reality other than the self. From there, it becomes more complicated. Other people begin to take their place within the framework of our lives. We slowly learn the system of checks and balances that grants us our freedom but, at the same time, sets limits where our freedom might otherwise encroach on the freedom of others.

We learn a love different from that which we first had for our parents, born, as it was in part, out of sheer necessity. There is a love that we have freely to give and a love that is freely given in return. We learn that we cannot coerce and manipulate without turning love into exploitation. But sometimes we do not arrive at that degree of detachment. We remain stuck in something that still resembles the perceptions of our infancy. We fail to detach people from our need of them, seeing them only as substitutes for the mother who gave us what we demanded, life and sustenance. We do not acknowledge that others have their own freedom and integrity and can themselves lay claims on our self-giving. It is that failure to distinguish others from ourselves that leads to insensitivity. Perhaps to protect ourselves from pain, or to conceal from ourselves the pain that we cause others, we grow a thick skin of cynicism, a world-weary imitation of true maturity.

Thirdly, we refuse to recognise that a greater familiarity with moral questions often leads to a reluctant admission of their complexity. Under the inner constraints of our own need for clear guidelines or in response to pressure from others to reduce all moral questions to acceptably simple equations, we deny the complexity and opt for simplistic generalisations. There are, indeed, moral convictions at

which we will arrive and which will prove to be fundamental to our view of life and the way we live it. The route
to those hard-won convictions lies through accepting
the complexity of most moral issues and not trying to
circumvent it. Whatever politicians may demand, moral
questions cannot be reduced to simplistic categories, where
black and white never shade into grey and slogans replace
hard-won convictions.

If we are to avoid these premature and sometimes permanent halts in our journey of faith, then much will depend
upon what we believe about God. Knowledge of God is
fundamental to all other knowledge. It provides the context
for everything else that we know. In a way, it is the goal
of all other knowledge. Yet it is not placed whole within
us at our conversion or at our baptism. Our earthly pilgrimage is one in which we enter ever more deeply into
God. There is always a dynamic relationship between our
life experience and what we believe about God. The truth
around which our lives revolve has the characteristic of a
rock-like stability, but is not inert or static. God is constantly encountering us. Our capacity for understanding
what he shows us and what he says to us increases with
time.

One of the reasons we call a premature halt to our
journey is that we invest everything in our past experience.
God is always to be found in what has already happened
because this cannot be questioned. But God is in our future,
as well. He does not passively wait for us to arrive where
he is, but calls us to find him in what is yet to be. The
past is only one dimension of the Christian life. Jesus
Christ, who is the same yesterday, today and forever, leads
us out of yesterday and today into the greater knowledge
of tomorrow.

Our relationship with God and what we believe about
him will determine the way we follow him and the expec-

tations that we have of him. It is this relationship which is fundamental to all others: the relationship with ourselves, with the church, with our neighbours and our enemies, and with the societies within which we live. For Christians, the God in whom they believe is the Father revealed in Jesus Christ, witnessed to within both the Hebrew and Christians Scriptures, proclaimed and sought by successive generations of the Church and known in our present experience through the work of the Holy Spirit.

Revelation, however, even the revelation that comes to us in Jesus Christ, is seen through our human eyes and coloured by our human expectations. Part of the work of pilgrimage is to sharpen our perception of Christ and, thereby, to understand and love more deeply the God whom he reveals to us. It is a task in which the Church has been engaged for the two thousand years of its history. Movements of renewal and reformation, or recovery and fresh insight, have been motivated by the desire to see Christ more clearly. The same sort of renewals, reappraisals and reformations have to take place in ourselves during the course of our lives.

We can, none of us, escape viewing God through the theological spectacles of that part of the Church to which we belong. Our experience within the Church will form the way in which we interpret our experience of God. Some have found their awareness of God awakened by sacraments, others by sermons, beginnings that can make the experience of one almost inaccessible to the other.

Different groups of Christians also use different vocabularies to express what they believe. Thus, we inherit words of which we are not the original authors. They aim to express the inexpressible and, through our life in the Church, become our possession, authenticating what we have experienced. They also exclude others whose experience of God begins in other environments and is described in different vocabularies. The Christian who describes herself as 'born again' often finds it hard to recognise any other language to account for the Christian experience of God and confuses the reluctance of other people to use that language with failure to know the experience of which it speaks.

Sometimes, if we are honest with ourselves, our denominational baggage is at odds with the way in which God is experienced in our lives. A gulf opens up between our view of God and the way we actually live. We may have been taught to believe in a God who views with profound distaste human beings whom he judges to be corrupt to the very core of their being. This will have little effect upon the way we live with our neighbours, however. We will still cherish decency and be disappointed when we fail to find it. We will still condemn churlishness and cruelty even though our theology affirms that we have no right to expect anything else. We may believe in a God who controls every detail of our daily lives and yet go to great pains to secure our personal happiness and to ensure our own survival. Yet, despite this distance between experience and the language that we use about God, we persist with the language and shape our view of God by it rather than by the way in which he is actually experienced.

In addition to the language that is part of our denominational legacy, we also find that there are words about God that seem to be the starting point of people of every denomination and of none. No matter what the fine detail of what we believe about God, there is a common consensus of shared assumptions as to what God is all about. There are certain qualities and attributes that cannot seriously be claimed by human beings and which, by contrast, therefore belong to the prerogative of divinity. For instance, it is taken for granted that any talk of God must include the assumption that he is omniscient, he knows everything, and that he is omnipotent, he is all-powerful. In the Greek tradition, from which we derive most of our language about divinity, there is also some further fine tuning. For instance, that God is immutable, he does not change, and that he is impassible, he does not suffer.

It is assumed that, if any one of these attributes were open to serious questioning, the whole notion of God would come tumbling about our ears. We cannot finally know whether God would survive any qualification of these divine absolutes, but we suspect that our religious faith would not. We need beliefs like this in order to be the religious people that we are. Omniscience is a form of knowledge that no one else can share, it is absolute. Religion sometimes, however, claims to provide an access for a select few into areas of knowledge concealed from the many. In the early decades of the Church, for instance, groups known as gnostics built a whole religion around the notion of secret knowledge possessed only by themselves. It was this knowledge, and just as much the fact that other people did not possess it, that gave them their identity not only as religious believers but also as human beings. Being privy to secrets has always been a means of enhancing personal status. To have suggested to the gnostics that God himself might impose limits on his own knowledge would have faced them with the threat that a measure of ignorance might also play its part in the divine ordering of things.

The need of a great deal of religious faith to believe that God is omniscient is surpassed only by the need to believe that he is omnipotent. For many, power is more important than knowledge, though knowledge is arguably a form of power. The idea of God's omnipotence suggests that God has infinite resources of power, can do whatever he likes, and is in complete control of everything that happens. The most ardent advocate of divine omnipotence would accept at least one qualification of that endless power and that is that God does not have the power to do evil. Though, it has to be said, Zwingli, one of the protestant reformers, believed that if God willed to do evil then, because he is God, it would no longer be evil.

As we shall have cause to recognise often in the pages that follow, power is probably the most seductive and manipulative ingredient in religious faith. Bound up with our belief that God is in complete control is the idea that we also, by believing in him and appropriating his power, might share that power and exercise far more control over our own lives and (who knows?) over the lives of other people as well. It was the glimpse of undreamed of power that prompted Simon the Sorceror to offer Peter and John money for the gift of passing on the Holy Spirit by the laying on of hands, a request that received the dusty answer it deserved.

Power has often been advocated by religion as a means of dealing with the world. It has been institutionalised and centred in the hands of the few who have thereby been able to control the many. It has been coveted as a means of rescuing individual men and women from the normal frailties of human experience and its possession sought as a talisman to ward off the evils of the world that are part of the common lot of others. To suggest that God imposes limits on his own power, or that God may not work by controlling everything that happens, would pose a threat to all those who cherish power in religion. It would admit that there are other ways that God chooses, that there are limits and parameters within which we all have to live, even that powerlessness might also be included in God's way of furthering his purposes. Further, it would challenge their right to control others.

Yet it is to such conclusions that a radical acceptance of God's revelation of himself in Jesus Christ may lead us. Christians believe that God makes himself known supremely in Jesus Christ. As Luther affirmed:

I know of no other God than he who was born of the Virgin Mary and who suffered and died upon the cross.

When they look at Jesus, Christians say, 'God is like this'.

Yet, too often that revelation in Jesus is made to confirm our existing ideas about God instead of challenging them.

Let us continue to use omniscience and omnipotence as examples. It will be argued that, since these attributes belong to God's essence, he cannot be God without them. Consequently, if Jesus reveals God to us, if he is the image of the invisible God, then he too must possess these attributes.

Thus, concealed beneath his humanity, Jesus knows everything. He will, in no way, be conditioned by the beliefs of the age in which he lives. His acceptance of demon possession as the cause of various forms of mental or physical illness obliges us to accept that interpretation ever after, regardless of the advances we make in our understanding of the human psyche. An omniscient redeemer would have known as much as any twentieth century psycho-analyst about the activity of the unconscious mind or the roots of neurotic behaviour and would have responded appropriately. The fact that he did not, and that he is omniscient, means that, backed by his omniscient authority, we are to go on believing in demons regardless of any advances in human self-knowledge. Whatever concessions we may make to Freudian insights, the demons are alive and well and likely to remain so.

In the gospel story, Jesus does not appear as all-knowing. He does not know who touched him in the crowd when the woman with a haemorrhage seeks for healing,[6] nor whether the disciples will leave him when the crowds begin to desert him,[7] nor the hour in which all things will finally be consummated.[8] Yet, this willingness not to know in no way detracts from his divine nature.

Likewise, Jesus does not present himself as omnipotent. He leaves Nazareth unable to perform any mighty works because of their unbelief.[9] The man at the pool of Bethesda has to want healing in order to receive it.[10] Disciples are called and invited into his service, not coerced.[11] When he is taunted and told to come down from the cross, the power that might wrench out the nails is subordinated to a greater power that keeps him secured by them.[12]

One explanation of this apparent acceptance of limitations to his knowledge and power is that Jesus divested himself of some of the attributes of God when he came to earth. Known as *kenoticism*, it is a view based on the Greek word used by Paul in Phillipians 2. 5–7:

> Let your bearing towards one another arise out of your life in Christ Jesus. For the divine nature was his from the first; yet he did not think to snatch at equality with God, but made himself nothing (*kenosis*), assuming the nature of a slave.

In the words of the Authorised Version of the Bible, he 'emptied himself'. This suggests that Jesus left behind, as it were, those attributes of divinity that could not easily be fitted into the framework of a human life. To be human is not to be omniscient or omnipotent. It involves a measure of ignorance, it requires us to live within boundaries that are given to us rather than marked out by us. Jesus, it may be said, by becoming incarnate was prepared to live with that ignorance and to accept a life circumscribed by those boundaries. There was a part of being God that he did not bring to earth; he renounced it for the sake of being truly human. Many Christians have seen this willingness to limit himself to the possibilities of our human life, to leave the infinite wealth of heaven for the finite poverty of earth, as a measure of his love towards us. That sense of astonishment remains with us, whatever judgment we may come to on the matter of *kenoticism*. As John Betjeman's poem reminds us during the Christmas season

> No love that in a family dwells
> No carolling in frosty air
> Nor all the steeple-shaking bells
> Can with this single truth compare -

That God was Man in Palestine
And lives today in Bread and Wine.[13]

Love and wonder will remain, even if we go on to question
whether the self-emptied Christ on earth leaves in heaven
a God who is much the same as we have always imagined
him to be. Theology has traditionally distinguished
between 'God in himself' and 'God for us'. A *kenotic* Christ
on earth, it is argued, is watched over by a God in heaven
who retains all the traditional attributes that we naturally
associate with him. Only so much of God could come down
to earth, the rest remains in heaven. In Christ, we see
something of God, but the rest is hidden from our sight.
The God who remains out of sight, as it were, retains
all those divine characteristics that humans have usually
believed God to possess. Our view of God remains essentially unchanged by that 'brief Galilean interlude', as the
philosopher Alfred North Whitehead described it. The God
that we see in Jesus, a God who, beyond all doubt, is love
and who accepts us as magnanimously and forgivingly as
the father accepted his prodigal son on his return from the
far country, has to be seen against the back-cloth of a God
in heaven who, to our eyes, remains essentially unchanged.
He is as we always imagined him to be. He is all-powerful
and all-knowing. If he were not, we believe, he would cease
to be God.

We end up doing a theological balancing act. It has
various permutations. There is the God of justice in heaven
who is placated by the revealed God of love on earth. There
is the holy God, in heaven, who hides himself from human
sin over against the Jesus who is the friend of publicans
and sinners on earth. There is the all-powerful God and
the crucified Christ. For some people, negotiating this high
wire has seemed preferable to the alternative of asking how
love affects our view of divine justice, how solidarity with
humankind in its sinfulness affects our view of divine holi-

ness and how divine power is to be understood in terms of the death of Christ.

Preferring to hold on to our traditional views of what God is like, there have been times when Christian theologians have portrayed Jesus as one who negotiates on our behalf with this God in heaven. Sometimes, because it fits well with omnipotence, the Father has been portrayed as a God who judges and condemns, a God who dispenses the power of life and death, a God who holds in his hands our destiny and decides our fate. In our human experience, there is no power more absolute than that.

Jesus has been portrayed as expressing a love that offers, and the Father as adhering to a righteousness that accepts, the sacrifice of bloody death upon the cross. It is as if the Father and the Son have acted out two roles, the Father as righteous judge and the Son as loving redeemer. Theology has, at times, been aware of the dangers in that sharp dichotomy. It has reminded us that the love revealed in Jesus has its source in God himself. It would be impossible to think otherwise. However, the love that is revealed has been presented as only one aspect of God, another side to his character, as it were. As such, it has to be balanced against the other attributes of God, those attributes such as omnipotence and omniscience which remain unrevealed because they cannot be contained within the parameters of a human life. Love, it is claimed, can. The conclusion that might so easily flow from this is that the 'hidden' attributes of God, which we cannot share, are more profoundly God-like than love, which we can.

There is another way, however. In this, we refuse to distinguish between 'God in himself' and 'God for us'. As we look at Jesus, we affirm our faith that this is indeed what God is like and that there is no other God, apart from the God seen in Jesus. He is a God who imposes limits upon his own knowledge and power in order that we might be truly free and might grow into a relationship with him which is truly that of sons and daughters.

He accepts limitations upon his knowledge, awaiting our yes or no when he calls us. He knows us profoundly, from the very womb of our mothers. He guides us, he sees before us the path that will lead to our truest happiness. Yet he is willing to wait upon our decisions, even to choose other routes to the fulfilment of his will when, in our foolishness, we thwart it.

He limits his power. He makes space for us to be truly free. He calls us. He waits for us, gathering our evasions and procrastinations into that infinite patience through which his will is done in the world.

In all this, God reveals to us in Christ that love is of the very essence of his being. Even as we accept that, in creation and redemption, God imposes limits on his knowledge and his power, so we affirm that there are no limits to this flaming, blinding, humbling and redeeming reality that lies at the heart of all things and that there is no greater miracle than that it should be contained in a human life. If that love which is revealed in Jesus is of the essence of God, then there is nothing 'left behind' that we need to know in order to fill out our picture of him. There, in Jesus, is the whole truth. All else that we wish to say about God has to be ordered by that truth, shaped in conformity with its pre-suppositions and subject to its sovereignty.

Accepting that as our starting point opens up other possibilities. Love is seen as God's supreme revelation of himself in Christ and a revelation that determines *everything* else that we believe about him. In Christ, God does not reveal a part of himself that has, somehow, to be reconciled with the other attributes that remain beyond our sight; he reveals his whole self. Rather than love, under the limiting circumstances of Christ's incarnation, having to be squared with all the other things that we believe about a God who does not have to accept those limitations, love shapes what we believe about the God beyond our sight.

There is one God. He is the God who came incarnate in the flesh of Jesus, was born in the straitened circumstances of Bethlehem, walked amongst us in Galilee, suffered on the cross for us at Calvary, and rose on the third day. There is not, on the one hand, a God who knows everything and can do anything and, on the other hand, a Christ who speaks of things that are not yet known and, in some situations, can act only where there is human faith, human partnership and human consent. There is one God who is love in heaven and on earth, and who therefore accepts limitations to his knowledge and places restrictions upon his power.

In the Incarnation, Jesus reveals to us the way in which God relates to humankind. That pattern of relationship is as true of God the Father, who remains beyond our sight, as it is of God the Son who is seen by us in Galilee. The manner of Christ's dealings with people does not arise simply out of the limitations set by the Incarnation; rather, it results from the way that God relates to his creation. Jesus did not coerce people, bending them to his will. He invited them into the way of discipleship. Some accepted his invitation, others turned away, either dismayed at his radical demands or distracted by matters they felt to be of greater importance. He stressed the primacy of faith, whether in the process of healing or people's perception of the kingdom of God by which they were surrounded. He relieved people neither of the burden of faith nor of decision. Here was no divinity that raised the weight of responsibility from human shoulders. He called men and women into a partnership.

Finally, he went to the cross, there to enter profoundly into human suffering and to bear the consequences of human sin. He set in the midst of human life a place where all future generations might most surely find God; this place so vulnerable, so full of pain where, armed only with love, faith and the willingness to obey the Father's purposes, he laid down his life. They proved to be the only weapons adequate to overcome the forces of evil. Earthly power would have met like with like, tyranny with tyranny, aggression with aggression, violence with violence. It was love that broke the chain reaction of destructive human power. It was faith that trusted all things to the Father's purposes, believing that darkness was the chosen rendezvous with light, that life would be brought out of death, that the total loss of Good Friday would result in the restoration of all things on Easter Sunday morning.

Yet, even the Resurrection followed the same pattern of invitation, the same call to faith and decision. The Resurrection accounts do not resonate with the sound of trumpets. There are doubts, hesitations, uncertainties, failures of understanding. The long journey to Emmaus is made without recognition of the Risen Christ who walks with the disconsolate travellers. Thomas is given the evidence he asks for, nail-pierced hands and wounded side, but told that there will be countless people who will come after him, for whom there will be no such evidence and no recourse save faith. Peter is invited to take a stroll on the beach and asked, again and again, if he is truly committed to love. Even at Olivet, the place of parting, the disciples ask questions and continue to be bemused by the meaning of the Kingdom.

The actions of Jesus are an expression of the nature of God. Jesus does not act in this way because he has to move within the temporal limitations imposed by the conditions of the Incarnation. Rather, his actions express what is *always* God's way with us. God does not coerce, he invites. He does not compel us to respond to his purposes, he gives us our freedom to respond or to turn away to other things. Because his freedom and ours are completely open to the future, we may even dare to say that just as he does not impose his will upon us, neither does he foresee our decisions. He knows the limited possibilities of any given situation, but he awaits our response within it. The route of his will might lie through the centre of our lives but, if we reject that high calling, he will turn to other ways, explore other possibilities, extend other invitations.

At the heart of all his dealings with us is an eternal love and an infinite patience. Omniscience could foresee every future decision and omnipotence ensure conformity to God's will. Instead, God calls us into partnership with himself, a partnership in which he accepts all the risks of our humanity. He knows our unreliability and capacity for stupidity, betrayal and meanness of spirit. He knows, as well, our ability, strengthened by his grace, to scale heights of courage and to go to lengths of loving that in our most sober moments we would deem to be beyond us. To this volatile human mixture he has entrusted the furtherance of his purposes in the world. It is from amongst humankind that he seeks his partners in achieving what he desires.

For some, this radical resolve to deal with God only as he is made known in Christ and to posit nothing of God that cannot also be said of Christ will be seen as a stripping of the divine assets. It will be construed as an act of theological effrontery, a humanist attempt to displace God from the centre of his universe. What is displaced, however, is not God but a view of God, a view no less human and no less motivated by human needs.

The God who is at the heart of all things is the God and Father of Our Lord Jesus Christ whose nature is love and whose goal is the reconciliation of all things through his everlasting mercy. From that affirmation flows all else that we would wish to say of God's justice, God's power, God's purposes. If we believe that love is inadequate to the task that God has set himself then we do not understand love. We are reading back into God not love as it is revealed in Christ but our own emasculated versions of it. For love is a consuming fire; it is the power, as Dante said, that moves the stars. It is love that judges us and strips us of our pretensions, sets light to our consciences, purges us of our sins and burns away our guilt. It is in the painful encounter with love that we truly see ourselves and learn, for the first

time, who we are. It is God's loving dealings with his
people that are remembered from the past, it is love that
sustains us in the present, it is love that calls to us out of
the future and sets before us the tasks to be done. It is love
that will come at the end, administering justice on behalf
of all the world's victims, revealing the whole terrible truth
of our inhumanity one to the other, consuming all that
knows no remorse, and finally gathering everything into
the unity of the Blessed Trinity.

The claim that all our dealings are with a God whose
name is love is no soft option. It is not an escape from
what are seen as the more rigorous demands of a God who
is aweful and terrible in his otherness. It is living with a
God who has already entered our human situation in Jesus
Christ and who is not to be expected to come galloping
over the hill like the Seventh Cavalry every time we send
up distress signals. It is realising that we are responsible
human beings and, like the prodigal son, we cannot escape
our vocation as the sons and daughters of God. He, returning from the far country, resolved that he would present
himself to his father in some other role. He would be a
servant and renounce the privileges of sonship. Son he was,
however, and coming back meant accepting again both the
privileges and responsibilities of sonship. It is knowing
that God having made the one, gracious decision for our
salvation, we are faced, day by day, with our own free
decision to do his will in the minute particulars of our lives.
It is recognising God's presence in the whole of life and
the impossibility of fencing off parts of life that belong to
his domain, leaving others unhallowed and untouched by
grace.

It is parts of that life which we are now to explore as
the growing points of our experience. Within them we shall
see how the inter-action of God's grace and our freedom is
the means by which God brings us to maturity. If it is not
a journey for the faint-hearted, neither is it for the self-
sufficient. It is a journey made in the company of the one

whom Julian of Norwich called 'our courteous Lord'. Our fellow pilgrims are men and women like ourselves, each with a journey never wholly replicated in the life of another, but each recognising in the others something of his or her own experience.

Notes

1 Ephesians 4.13.
2 1 Corinthians 13.12.
3 Hebrews 13.14.
4 1 John 1.1.
5 Julian of Norwich *Showings* (Classics of Western Spirituality (London: SPCK 1978) pp. 274–275).
6 Luke 8.43–8.
7 John 6.67.
8 Matthew 24.36.
9 Matthew 13.58.
10 John 5.6.
11 Luke 5.1–11, 27–28.
12 Luke 23.35.
13 John Betjeman *Collected Poems* (London: John Murray, 1958) p. 190.

Chapter Two

Growth Through Prayer

Theology and prayer are inseparable. Neither should be allowed to become a substitute for the other. There can be theology that, by stopping short of prayer, keeps itself at one remove from God himself. The longing for God which, as the Psalmist said, is like a deer longing to slake its thirst at a brook, is replaced by words. We forget what Thomas Aquinas taught us centuries ago, that words are analogies, they try to approximate to the truth, to come as close as human words ever can to saying what God is like. Behind them there is the reality of God himself who bursts out of words. He is the one, eternal being for whom even the best and truest of all our words only act as symbols. They are something approaching the truth, they can never be the truth itself.

When we forget that, we are no longer driven to prayer. Holding in our hands a picture of the beloved, we confuse the image with the reality. Our ideas, our doctrines, our views of God, all do service for the reality of God himself. Thus, what should be one of the greatest enterprises of all, the making of a theology, becomes an empty exercise. We build 'follies', places remarkable for their style, their ingenuity, their imagination, but uninhabited. We build a city of words, but it is not like the city of God where each man sits beneath his vine and the sound of children's laughter is heard in the streets and God himself is the lamp and sun of it. Instead, it is a place where the streets echo to

the sound of our own voices and where there is to be found
no living centre on which all else converges. The quest of
true theology is to know God in himself. So understood, a
theologian (and it is a calling open to anyone who attempts
to say something about God) is one who will see all his or
her thinking and reflecting as a step towards a deeper
union with God.

There is also a form of prayer that, smugly alas, believes
that a hallmark of true spirituality is to despise theology.
Turning its back on a study of the Bible that discloses
anything but what we want to hear, shunning the words
of saints, martyrs, prophets and doctors of the Church,
rising above the man-made opinions of others, it cosily
ensconces itself with God as he is imagined to be. One's
own experience becomes the bench-mark by which everything is judged. Other people's experience, if it differs from
our own, is viewed as a threat instead of offering the potential of enlarging our own vision. If there is danger in
making words the substitute for the truth, there is a perhaps even greater danger of bypassing words and making
ourselves the substitute for truth.

In prayer, be it articulated in words or experienced in
silence, we are brought face to face with the God in whom
we believe. We evade that encounter by communing with
our theological or experiential images of him. Prayer itself
brings us to the God who stands beyond the words and is
far greater than anything that can be contained within our
own experience.

It is an encounter that takes place in the worship of the
Church, whenever we pray together with other Christians.
The liturgy of the Church is a good place to pray. It
is redolent with the language of the centuries. We are
surrounded not only by people, here and now, doing
exactly the same as we are doing, but also by the communion of saints and the great company of angels and
archangels.

In some traditions that shared experience of prayer is as

pervading as the incense lingering in the air. In other very different traditions it is audible in the murmured 'Amens', the reassuring sound of other people's consent to what is being said. In others, prayer is offered in a silence that becomes a physical and spiritual component of the place where we kneel. In others, in songs and hymns, love and faith are poured out. In the majority, when bread is broken and wine is uplifted, Christ is amongst us and we are surrounded by the surging presence of his people seen and unseen.

Liturgical prayer, prayer offered with other people, forms the basis of our life of prayer. No more than our words or experiences, however, should it be allowed to become a substitute for the one-to-one encounter of personal prayer.

We soon learn the difficulties of personal prayer. There are no other voices to sustain us when our words run dry. We are without the reassuring presence of other people who seem to be aware of God's nearness when we are not. We are thrown back upon our own resources. With nothing outside ourselves to distract us, we become conscious of the seething busyness of our minds.

There are ways of using this time. There are well-worn paths that lead to God. We read the Scriptures and meditate on what we have read, letting our minds rove freely through the scriptural stories. For some, there is the rosary, with its constant recalling of the joyous, sorrowful and glorious mysteries of our faith. For others, the daily office, with its nurturing diet of psalm and prayer. All of us, however, are at some point left with our own words and our own silences. It is then that we begin to wait.

A great deal of prayer consists of waiting. There are no rapid routes to success in prayer. Daily prayer is not like the daily newspaper, a succession of communiques and news items describing a world moving on under the constantly changing banners of today's headlines. In Christian prayer, the headlines are always the same, proclaimed in the Eucharist of the Church

Christ has died
Christ has risen
Christ will come again!

The consequence of those momentous truths for ourselves are painstakingly written in the small print of our unfolding lives. Slowly, joyously and painfully, our journey to maturity takes us into a deeper understanding of, and deeper communion with, the God whom we love and confess. But the journey will not be hurried. We have to learn that prayer keeps to a tempo different from the brisk rhythms of our daily life. And, at the heart of it, we are waiting for God. Even when we are utterly persuaded of his presence, even in those moments when we know ourselves enfolded in his love, even then we cannot compel him to speak nor quicken the pace at which he goes about his purposes.

Prayer teaches us not to associate God inevitably with the dramatic and breath-taking. Such moments there may be: we may have our Damascus Road, our Pentecosts, our Mount Olivets and remember them long years after they have happened. But our growing knowledge of God is not formed out of a succession of action replays of those events. They are signposts, setting us in the right direction. It is the journey itself that is important. The long days and months when there is no blinding light, no sound of a mighty, rushing wind, no vistas seeing clear to the gates of heaven itself. They are the days of companionship. Walking with God and learning what only time, waiting and listening can teach us. The most cursory glance at the history of the Church should teach us that God works in centuries not in decades.

The *andante* of prayer may disturb or even embarrass us. It does not seem to keep pace with our thinking about God. We handle biblical words and theological ideas with growing assurance, but prayer makes us painfully aware that we do not know God as deeply as our words would suggest. Behind our growingly articulate ability to conceptualise God, we hide our unwillingness to pray to him. The silence of the one-to-one encounter makes us realise that we know less than we claim we know, the union of our hearts with the living God has not yet arrived where our words are. We are baffled by the poverty of our faith and the meagreness of our spiritual resources. The temptation is to live on a diet of ideas. It is easy to succumb. Concepts of God have always had the power to seduce people into believing that to know them is to know the reality of which they speak.

It is at this point that we face what is first demanded of us if we will grow to maturity. It is discipline. Discipline is a notion that will be greeted with enthusiasm by some and abhorrence by others. Both attitudes deserve only our suspicion. The spiritual disciplinarian would have us quickly locked into a method of prayer that becomes an end in itself. The method becomes everything. It may be imposed upon us before we are ready for it or trap us long after it has ceased to serve any useful purpose in our spiritual life. The spiritual libertarian will scorn any structure at all and have us encountering God everywhere, in the world of nature or the depth of human relationships, but never consistently in that painful one-to-one encounter of personal prayer.

Discipline does not mean slavish adherence to particular forms of prayer. Forms, like the Sabbath, were made for people, not people for the forms. Like the Sabbath, they are necessary in providing rhythm to our lives and opportunity for silence and reflection. The form of prayer should, however, be the shoes of our spiritual journey. It should fit and be comfortable. We have to learn to be resistant to enthusiastic disciplinarians who would shoe our feet in footwear of their choosing. There is nothing to compel us to wear seven-league boots that are too heavy and large for us, or be forced into exotic silver slippers which we have to fit into in order to establish our identities. We are

neither spiritual giants nor cinderellas having to compete
with others for royal favours. Neither should one form be
expected to do us service for a lifetime. We may begin our
prayer life with chatty quiet times, move on to the well-
ordered paths of the breviary or daily office, use this book
or that, and finally return to the place where we began.
Prayer is like that voyage of discovery described by T. S.
Eliot:

> We shall not cease from exploration
> And the end of our exploring
> Will be to arrive where we started
> And know the place for the first time.[1]

This selective approach to the forms of prayer is not to
be confused with spiritual *laissez-faire*, however. If God
is consistently to be found in the one-to-one of human
relationships, we have to wait for him in the one-to-one
encounter of prayer. No, he will not abandon us if we do
not pray. The world is full of his grace and we shall find
him in the poor, the sick, the outcast, the oppressed; we
shall find him in the unfolding miracle of nature; we shall
find him in a Mozart symphony or a Barbra Streisand song
– but, behind all the gifts, there is the giver. It is his
features that we must learn to recognise if we are to hear
what the poor are saying and be of any use to them. It is
on his face that we must steadfastly gaze if we are to look
unflinchingly at the world of nature when the rain does
not come in the areas of famine, or virul syndromes are
spawned over which we have no control. It is his voice we
need to listen to when the most beautiful music has fallen
silent and human eloquence reached its limits.

Discipline is the willingness to go back, day by day, to
the place where we wait for God. The chief virtue of any
method of prayer should be that it encourages us to lay
our lives open before God and come face to face with him.
Prayer is not a discipline that will go away from us. If we

put it on one side, for days or for weeks, sometimes for months or for years, God will not harass us or nag us, nor even hide himself from us. But we will know – like a member of family knowing that letters, phone calls, even Interflora flowers, are becoming a way of evasion, keeping at a distance what should be seen, held and shared – we will know that there is a closeness to God that will come by prayer and by no other way.

It is in waiting, or in returning after a period of absence in prayer, that the importance of what we believe about God becomes apparent. We may fall prey to frustration or intimidation if we do not know him aright. The frustration will cut short the time we are willing to wait. A God of power, we believe, should be able to cut a swathe through the entanglements of time and adverse circumstances in order to do what he wants to do and say what he has to say. We do not have the patience of Simeon who, only after a lifetime of waiting and praying, at the eleventh hour held in his arms the object of all his longings. Only when nothing remained except to ask that he might depart in peace, did his eyes see the salvation for which he had prayed so long. Such waiting is possible only if we believe that God is not capricious but as faithful as the distant hills.

Likewise, a sense of intimidation will hold us back from returning to prayer when we have been too long away from it. If God's first words are to be words of rebuke, if we cannot see beyond the need to acknowledge unreliability in the face of his omnipotence, then we shall not hasten home. Yet we can better judge the mood of the waiting father than could the prodigal son when he set out on his journey. We know, because we have heard it time and again, that the Father awaits us and will see us coming whilst we are still a long way off, and there will be no lectures, no searching questions about where we have been,

only the Father's house ringing with songs of homecoming.
Sometimes we are detained in the far country of prayerless-
ness not because we lack a profound desire to be home but
because, even having heard the Gospel a hundred times,
we still cannot truly accept that God is infinite mercy and
grace.

Waiting and returning would be less difficult if we were
to accept that what God has said to us in Jesus Christ is
the truth, the whole truth and nothing but the truth. We
would not be dismayed that we have to wait so long if we
recognised that God revealed himself most profoundly by
hiding himself in the stuff of our human life. Here, there
are no unchanging and unalterable patterns of revelation.
It is a place where plans go awry, notorious for the inaccur-
acy of its communications between people who see what
they want to see and hear what they want to hear. It is
small wonder that the Devil tried to persuade Jesus that
leaping from the parapets of the Temple into the arms of
waiting angels was a far more reliable way of carrying out
his mission.

Forty days Jesus wrestled with that temptation. And
for almost as many months he trod his way through the
conflicting religious expectations and steaming politics of
his time on his way to the cross. There were six hours in
his dying. Three days in the tomb, the disciples unaware
that all creation was waiting for the third day. Forty days
he came and went among them. And, since then, almost
two thousand years seeing the travail of his soul in the
ebb and flow of human events, the painful rejections, the
glorious achievements, the consistent discipleship of countless men and women whose unremembered names will not
be known until the end of the world.

Within that context, it is a small thing to wait in prayer.
Such waiting is, in part, a focusing of our spiritual sight.
A moment comes, our blurred vision at last clarified, when
we see him where he always is, hidden in this human place
where the unfolding of his eternal purposes is not to be

confused with the breathless, transient plans that we make from day to day.

In Jesus, too, we find the confidence to return when he has waited long for us. The mystics of the Church have used paradigms of prayer that have suggested journeying. The anonymous author of the *Cloud of Unknowing* speaks of the ascent of a mountain where the summit is wrapped in cloud and the past lies below, concealed beneath the mists of forgetting. The Cloud where God dwells is not to be defined, contained within our knowledge in such a way that we convince ourselves that we possess it. There is nothing that will pierce the Cloud save darts of love, flying swiftly to their target in the confidence that God is known by love because he is love himself.[2] Julian of Norwich, granted visions of the crucified Christ, crowned with thorns, journeyed twenty years in prayer allowing the meaning of what she had seen to unfold within her. It was a journey in which her confidence increased with each step, knowing that the God who had spoken in Jesus was utterly to be trusted. Mother, as well as Father, he held her, in gentleness and strength, like a hazelnut resting in the palm of his hand.[3] St John of the Cross called men and women to the austerity of the active night of the senses in which the soul would be overtaken by a night far deeper. Yet, he never failed to believe that, when we were reduced to nothing except 'naked faith', we would be as bride to the bridegroom, sharing the nuptials of everlasting love.[4] In such journeyings the human spirit, sometimes encountering inauspicious auguries along the way, will not be dissuaded from its purpose if it holds constantly to the belief that God is all that he has revealed himself to be in Jesus.

The simplicity of believing that all things are to be found in Christ is the point to which maturity brings us, not the starting point from which our journey begins. As sudden and stark as our initiation into Christ may be, like Bunyan's Pilgrim we continue to carry, some distance into our journey, the baggage of the life we are leaving. Signifi-

cantly, it was after faith and conversion that Pilgrim came
at last to the cross where the burden fell from his back.

It is the cross that alone can strip us of the stubborn
presuppositions with which we begin our pilgrimage. We
may imagine that, by becoming Christian, we have
divested ourselves of the crippling neuroses and imperious
sins that have hitherto played such a part in our lives. In
our hearts, we may refuse to acknowledge their persistent
presence, instead affirming the power of God to change
us, quickly and painlessly. So power becomes a necessary
attribute of God because, in some way, it is bound up with
our own self-esteem. We cannot go on deceiving ourselves,
however. In repentance and conversion we have simply
changed direction. There is a new grace in our lives that
was not there before. But the work of renewing our being,
what the New Testament calls sanctification, is only just
beginning. It is a long process of change in which we slough
off, layer by layer, the comfortable clothing of our former
sins and failures. It is a process of simplification, the simpli-
fying of our person. In its course, our ideas of God must
also be simplified.

The work of sanctification is a gradual work of self-
recognition, self-acceptance and increasing surrender to
God's good grace. It is one in which our partnership with
God is essential. God does not place his hands over our
eyes so that we cannot see or understand the inner work
of renewal that is taking place within us. Our own response
and consent to what is happening is essential to the enterpr-
ise. That is why the cross is central to our growth in grace;
for there we realise that there is a real death involved in
the gift of resurrection; there we realise that God is power
insofar as he is love and through his patient love and our
response to it, renewal is possible. We learn that although
miracles may happen in a moment, moral and spiritual
renewal takes a little longer.

Prayer is a journey drawing us closer to God and deepening our self-understanding. It is also an expression of compassion. In the one-to-one relationship of personal prayer, the very process of being drawn into deeper communion with God brings us closer to others. This will find its expression in intercession.

The prayer for others holds an important place within the corporate prayer life of the Church. It is part of the obligation of the Church, as the priestly body of Christ, to offer prayer on behalf of others. The Church stands in an intermediary role between God and his world. It represents the world to God and God to the world. This priestliness is not confined to a special order within the Church, it is the calling of all who walk the Christian way. In its prayers, the Church fulfils its priestly calling by bearing before God the needs, the hopes, the sorrows, the dilemmas and diseases of the human race. The individual Christian is part of that ministry and that ministry forms part of his or her life. When we gauge the place of prayer in our lives, account has to be taken of the offering of intercession, made alongside other Christians, whether in the liturgy of the church or in smaller prayer groups.

It is an offering that we also make as individuals, however. The journey of self-understanding in personal prayer highlights our relationships to other people and the ways in which we express our concern for them. We come to realise that intercessory prayer is not the last desperate resort of people who find that their own interventions of caring love are losing their efficacy. It is recognising that the burden we bear is the burden that God bears and that he carries both the carer and the cared for. Our willingness to accept love's burden is strengthened by the realisation that we walk in partnership with God, able to love because we are loved by him, drawing on resources that last long after our own have dried up.

Intercessory prayer will pose demanding questions about the sort of God we believe in. The New Testament describes two ways in which God responds to human need and answers our human prayers.

The first, and the rarer of the two, is through miracle. Miracles play an important part in the Gospel story. It is their significance for future generations of Christians that baffles us. Some would claim that they set a new pattern in God's relationship with his creation. Christ lays before us a whole new range of possibilities, a pattern of divine intervention around which we can build our hopes. Certainly, the early Church discovered that miracles happened, as prison doors were opened, cures were effected and ills healed. There have been miracles in the long story of the Church ever since, appearing erratically and without respect for the churchmanship or theological allegiance of those involved in them. The stories of the saints echo with them, the waiting thousands at Lourdes have no doubts as to their possibility, a charismatic prayer group fervently prays for them.

Some believe that miracles would take their place within the day-to-day experience of Christian people more often, if only the right conditions were observed. These are various. Miracles would happen if only Christians prayed more, if they received the Holy Spirit, if they had more faith, if their lives were right with the Lord. The list always lays a burden of guilt on that vast majority of Christians for whom miracles seem strangely elusive. For an absence of miracles can then only be the symptom of shortcomings in prayer, an indifference to the Holy Spirit, a dearth of faith or a limping walk with the Lord.

It is a view that is dependent upon a particular view of God. His is a God who is outside the situations for which we pray and is persuaded to intervene. He is a God whose chief attribute is power. But he is also a God to whose counsels only the few are privy. Miracles stubbornly refuse to materialise as the legacy of the many. They are the prerogative of the few who possess the right key to open the door of God's blessing, know the right words and can

strike the right attitudes. There is another tradition in the
New Testament and within the Church. In St John's
gospel, the six miracles recorded are all referred to as
signs. They point to something greater and more important
beyond themselves. If Jesus fed five thousand in the wilderness, the lesson to be learned was not that, time and again,
he would feed hungry crowds in some Judean wilderness,
but that he would feed countless men and women with the
never-failing food of his body and blood.[5] When Jesus
raised Lazarus from the dead, it was not to introduce
us to a new way of circumventing death, summoning an
unending stream of beloved brothers, dead Lazaruses, from
the cold tomb in generations to come. It was a sign of the
third day when Christ would rise and of the last day when
all would be raised in him.[6]

In the story of the New Testament church, if there were
prison doors that opened, there were others that remained
firmly shut. Paul, more than once, referred to the hazards
and trials of the apostolic life, from floggings to the ignom-
iny of escaping in a basket. If there have been saints who,
by God's grace have performed miracles, they have also
warned us against too great a reliance upon them. St John
of the Cross was in no doubt

As for (their) temporal benefit, supernatural works, and
miracles merit little or no joy of soul. When the (spiritual) benefit, i.e. *knowledge and love of God caused by these
works*, is excluded they are of little or no importance to
man, since they are not in themselves means of uniting
the soul with God, as is charity.[7]

Miracles are a mystery to which, as with all mysteries,
our minds and hearts should remain open. They are not
the profoundest of mysteries, however, nor the basis upon
which we build our perception of God and his nature. The
greatest mystery of all is that the Word should have been
made flesh and that God should have concealed himself in

our humanity. It is a mystery that remains central to our lives as we continue to experience his risen presence, through the Holy Spirit, within the world, and in the minute particulars of our own lives.

It is sensitivity to this presence that we remember most of all in the lives of the saints. Most remembered is not Francis of Assisi's power to heal the leper, but his willingness to embrace him; we remember his songs and his joy in following Christ but, equally, we remember that love pierced his hands, feet and side. For every one person healed miraculously at Lourdes, there are countless pilgrims for whom there are no miracles. Yet these return glorifying and praising God, possessed of a deeper trust in God's purposes and a stronger awareness of his presence with them.

We should not place in conflict with each other the experience of miracle and the hidden experience of grace. But we should recognise that the former has happened only to a tiny minority in the annals of the Christian story, a recognition that neither denies miracles, nor prevents them from happening. They will happen as they have always happened and there will be no consistent reason for it. Miracles are a mystery.

In intercessory prayer, openness to miracle is superseded by openness to love and to all the possibilities of God's will. Far from invoking God to come into the situations for which we pray, intercession requires us to recognise his presence within them already. Before ever we pray, he has already responded to the needs that we bring before him. He is with the prisoner of conscience, the suffering friend, the casualty of racial violence, the victim of the terrorist's hate, the anxious relative, the hurt and bewildered partner of a broken marriage. Cast the net of prayer as widely as we will, he will be there.

It is the Incarnation itself and not the miracles that most reveal God. In Jesus, we see God's way of relating to us. The Gospel story is about people either seeing or failing to see. As John's story of Christ's healing of the man born blind tells us, more important than physical sight is the faith to discern the Son of Man. Blindness is no impediment to such seeing faith, nor is perfect vision a guarantee of it. Even where miracles occurred, many people failed to see the true purpose of them and to believe because of them. Jesus came to see that it was a wicked and unbelieving generation that continually asked for signs and more signs.[8]

It was his life amongst us that was the one abiding sign. To those who perceived it, to be in the presence of Christ was to be in the presence of God. When he spoke a word of forgiveness then nothing was left in earth or heaven to stand between the sinner and the God in heaven whose forgiving love Jesus declared. For the generations to come, faith has been aroused, not by Bartimaeus' opened eyes nor Jairus' daughter called to life, but by the cross and Resurrection. There is nowhere where God is more hidden, nowhere more bereft of miracle and grace, than the cross of Calvary. Yet here, the veil of the temple is torn apart and we see the beating heart of God that lies at the centre of all things. Here we know that there is no pain on earth that is not touched by God's presence, no hell into which he does not descend, no soul so desperate that it will not hear from the lips of Christ the promise of paradise.

The Resurrection does not release us from the burden of faith, either, as Jesus reminded Thomas. The doubting disciple was given his request for visible evidence of the risen Christ, but the generations to come would see what he had seen by faith alone. The accounts of the Resurrection do not reverberate with triumphalism and quick assurance. Jesus comes and goes strangely and unexpectedly. An upper room, a dusty road, a beach; the late evening, the early morning; these are the places and times of his coming.

God has not substituted for this way of disclosing himself the razzmatazz of the travelling salesman, here one day and gone the next. He is still hidden in all our situations and sometimes seen most clearly in those places most like Calvary. If indeed, the gift of life comes out of the willingness to die, whether to oneself, or to the world, or reluctantly to the belief that everything should revolve around our expectations of how things should be, then it is where the darkness is deepest that his renewing and life-giving presence is discovered.

Is intercessory prayer, then, only the recognition of God's presence in those situations for which we pray? Is it the case that prayer is needed, not to affect God, but to change ourselves? Are we the chief beneficiaries of our prayers for others? Again, we must look to Christ. In him, we realise that God has not established a coercive order within his universe, compelling us to do his will. His way is the way of partnership. As he calls us to share with him in his work of renewing creation, so he patiently allows his purposes to unfold in the world. Because he is infinitely patient, he waits for our assent and suffers the setbacks of our unbelief and our failures. Where we offer to him our love, a love that he himself has set within us and awakened, there his love in the world is increased.

The people for whom we pray are surrounded by Christ's presence and ours, by his love and ours. Where we offer faith, new possibilities emerge. Faith is active and dynamic, making possible what might not otherwise have happened. The partnership of prayer demonstrates that there is neither self-containment on God's side nor passivity on ours. He does not carry out his purposes, hidden in the world, regardless of our prayers and with no need of our Christian obedience. He who taught us to pray that God's will might be done on earth was telling us that the coming of God's kingdom had something to do with our praying for it.

Prayer is not a work that ministers only to our own souls and focuses our own perceptions, it is an active work of redemption and renewal. It may be that God could have achieved his will in other ways. The divine purposes could

have made a detour of the human and, far more quickly
and reliably, achieved their chosen ends. There was, however, no such detour. The central thrust of God's purposes
was made through the man Christ Jesus, his life, his
betrayal, his suffering and his resurrection. It is in the same
arena of the human that God continues to carry forward
his purposes.

Intercessory prayer is constantly dogged by the problem
of 'answered' and 'unanswered' prayer. When we think in
terms of God 'answering' our prayers, we forget that prayer
is itself an answer to God. His is always the initiative and
his the first word that is spoken. When we pray, we reply
to God. The word that has been spoken has been spoken
in Jesus Christ, so prayer is always a 'yes' and 'Amen' to
that word. Prayer is a statement of faith that God is present
in the world in the way that he has shown himself to be
present in Jesus. Therefore, in praying we know that God
shows himself in ways ranging from miracles to the cross.

We shall see him most clearly in what does not pass for
the miraculous: in the courage with which men and women
face suffering; in the tenacity with which they cling to what
they believe in the face of hostility; in the willingness of
the victim to forgive his or her violator; in the reconciliation
that heals the running wounds of division; in selflessness;
in the unquenchable enthusiasm of the young and the
battle-scarred wisdom of the old; in the patient work of
healing and the steady rehabilitation of those whom life
has broken; in the grit and determination of men and
women with physical disabilities; in words that comfort; in
a touch that reassures; in the smile of a Downs' syndrome
child. And there will be times when we see none of these
things. For, way beyond our sight, in the darkness that
sometimes enshrouds those whom the world violates so
cruelly, in the twilight world where no words of ours can
reach someone's mental pain, there will be a transaction
between God and the one whom we cannot reach. There
will be no evidence of a Risen Christ standing there in hell,

with all hell's victims. But faith will trace the marks of his suffering, as Thomas traced the print of the nails. If there is no end to our loving in prayer, then we should not have to persuade ourselves that there can be no end to God's.

Because these are the fruits of prayer, there will be times when we shall see what our faith and love have helped to make possible. That is love's reward. We may begin by calling it 'answered' prayer, but that is another way of saying that we have visible evidence of God's presence in the events for which we pray. There will come a point in our journey when we shall know that, whether we 'see' or not, God is there. An absence of prayer does not lead to an absence of God, but it does leave the world that much less touched by love and faith.

The phrase 'absence of God' is a chilling one. There have been times when theologians, thinking to make hell more hospitable and its provisions for the wicked less grotesque, have described it as 'an absence of God'. If the words are given their due weight, then hell so described is no less forbidding than our feverish imaginings of it. The absence of God is where the stricken cry out, 'My God, my God, why hast thou forsaken me?' Since that cry descended from the crucified Christ, however, there is no hell where he is not present. He has gathered all our hells into his own experience and broken their power in the Resurrection . . . 'he descended into hell; on the third day, he rose again from the dead'.

There will be times when life as we experience it, or the adversities of others, as we observe and try to make sense of them, will seem to be nothing less than an absence of God. That it is not so will be more an affirmation of faith than a true testimony to what we feel. Whatever our believing mind may tell us, in the pit of the stomach there will be felt a churning dread that God is absent. Faith does not become atheism, for that would be the simplest and least convincing way out. To cease believing would remove all contradictions. Faith chooses to affirm God's gracious purposes when that affirmation seems to fly clear in the face of all the available evidence and to trust in his presence even when he appears to leave no footprints for us to follow.

We should not be dismayed for we are in well-charted country. The experience of God's absence has been described from Augustine to Luther, from St John of the Cross to Thérèse of Lisieux, from the survivors of the holocaust to Bonhoeffer.

St John of the Cross traced the experience in his theology of prayer, calling it 'the dark night of the soul'. In many ways, he is one of our most reliable guides through the experience, if only because he enables us to bear it with hope. For him, it is an inescapable stage in the journey of prayer. Yet, it can be claimed, it was not borne simply out of his reflections on the contemplative life; it had its roots in the winter of 1578–9 when he was incarcerated in a Toledo cell by his brothers of the Carmelite order. It was out of that betrayal and suffering that he wrote his poem *The Dark Night*. It was only later that he spelt out its meaning for the life of prayer. The dark night, he said, is the place where we are stripped of everything, except 'naked faith', where we know our emptiness and that nothing will fill it save God himself. It is when we have come to this place that we stand on the threshold of a knowledge of God deeper than anything we have known before:

> On that glad night,
> In secret, for no one saw me,
> Nor did I look at anything,
> With no other light or guide
> Than the one that burned in my heart;

> This guided me
> More surely than the light of noon

To where he waited for me
– Him I knew so well –
In a place where no one else appeared.

O guiding night!
O night more lovely than the dawn!
O night that has united
The Lover with his Beloved,
Transforming the beloved in her Lover.[9]

It may be that, in the times of what seems to be God's absence, the words of a mystic or even the words of Scriptures themselves, will do little to assuage the pain. We may protest that there are other routes to maturity, other ways of knowing, preferable to this. Like the psalmist, we seem to see all around us people who are spared, living out a succession of cloudless days, Maybe – though we would be unwise to speculate on what lies behind the mask of someone else's public persona. We may resent having to tread such flinty ground and find the companionship of a saint, noted for his spiritual austerity, little or no comfort. It is certainly a stretch of our way that we would not have chosen and not everyone would be comforted by an assurance that God had chosen it for us. It is, however, where we are and it is out of these 'God-forsaken' experiences that we may discover just how deep is our need of God and how profound is his love for us.

The rewards of prayer far outstrip the price that has to be paid in terms of faith and commitment. Yet they do not come instantly packaged. There is a price to be paid. For true maturity, there always is.

Notes

1   T. S. Eliot 'Little Gidding' (*The Oxford Book of Twentieth Century Verse* (London: Oxford University Press 1973) p. 257).

2 Chapter VI *The Cloud of Unknowing* (Ed. J. Walsh *Classics of Western Spirituality* (London: SPCK 1981) pp. 130–31).

3 Julian of Norwich *Showings* p. 183.

4 St John of the Cross *The Spiritual Canticle* (*The Collected Works of St John of the Cross* (Washington: ICS Publications 1979) pp. 410f).

5 John 6.35.

6 John 11.25.

7 St John of the Cross *Ascent III.30.4* (Collected Works) p. 267.

8 John 9.1–41.

9 St John of the Cross *The Dark Night*, Stanzas 3–5 (*Collected Works*) pp. 295–96.

Chapter Three

Growth through the Church

Since the dawn of the Christian faith, becoming a disciple of Jesus has meant becoming a member of his Church. Jesus gathered around him a disparate group of men and women and formed them into the nucleus of the Church. Their nearness to him and to one another led to tensions and rivalries. Their natural leader, Peter, was a man of quick insight, prone to behaviour that could be impulsive and embarrassing to the rest. John, the one whom Jesus loved as the author of the fourth Gospel tells us, joined his brother James in laying claim to high ranking positions in the coming kingdom. Thomas was subject to doubt and pessimism. Judas betrayed Jesus. Alongside them were the women, though the New Testament narrative only occasionally raises the curtain on them. They were passionate in their loyalty to Jesus, capable of differences and not always listened to.

The Church that grew out of this nucleus inevitably increased the wealth of human potential, added to the tensions and produced people who ranged from the great to the eccentric. Some were both great and eccentric. What has been inescapable for any Christian through the centuries has been the need to come to terms with belonging to the Church. There are no options. Baptism is not an individual consent to a personal experience of salvation. It is a great deal more than the evangelical definition of a Christian as one who has accepted the Lord Jesus Christ as a personal saviour. Baptism marks our birth into a community with which we share our spiritual experience. It gifts us with brothers and sisters who are our family not by our choice, but by God's. They may or may not be people with whom we have a natural affinity, they are our kinsfolk in faith.

The Church presents us with both the greatest opportunity to attain maturity and the greatest test of it. What the New Testament seems to take for granted is that those who are made members of the Church have maturity required of them. The biblical images of the Church are far removed from the paternalism that has too often characterised the reality of our life together. They infer a readiness to accept responsibility and willingness to grow on the part of those who are its members.

A closer look at three of those images will illustrate the point.

There is the image of the body, employed to great effect by St Paul in 1 Corinthians 12. It is a living body whose health and effectiveness depend upon the balance, the inter-action and the functioning of every part. It is a democratic body that Paul portrays, in the sense that every member accepts some responsibility for the whole. If any part of the body is cut off then the pain affects the whole. Any part that does not function properly influences the effectiveness of the whole. There are many different functions, some a great deal more exalted than others, but none is dispensable or to be despised.

Paul could be said to be rejecting two models of the Church that have typified two ends of the Christian spectrum. The one is the model of hierarchy. In this, members gain in importance the nearer they come to the head. The lesser members, instead of playing a role of equal importance for the health of the whole, are defined in terms of their dependance on the stronger members. This runs counter to Paul's image, where even those parts of the body that we would discreetly conceal have their part to play.

The second model is the sectarian model. This holds

that the Church is in some way enriched by a constant process of fragmentation. Or, to change the metaphor, the body is made more effective by frequent amputations. Neither presents us with a desirable route to maturity. The one will not let us come of age. The other tries to settle family quarrels by storming out of the house and slamming the door.

A second image is found in 1 Peter 2. It is the image of the royal priesthood. The whole community, the holy people, fulfil the function of priesthood. The Church is an intermediary between God and the world. In its life and preaching it represents God to the world and, in its prayers, it represents the world to God. In priestly prayer it carries a wounded humanity, holding it before God and bearing it with God.

The Protestant reformers believed that all Christians shared responsibility for that work of priesthood. There were not full-time Christians and part-time Christians. There were not Christians who chose a high road to the kingdom, leaving their brothers and sisters to make the best they could of a low road paved with secular preoccupations. All were called, they believed.

We do not today have to take the whole reformation package. Martin Luther, deeply affected by his disturbing and frustrating experience as an Augustinian monk, believed that none were called to live the contemplative life. Today, both Protestants and Catholics recognise how powerfully the Church has been influenced and blessed by those who have given themselves to the celibate life of poverty, chastity and obedience. But the fact that some are called to celibacy does not diminish either the calling of marriage or a life of singleness in a secular setting. Men and women who make prayer the first commitment of their lives do not thereby devalue the prayers of those who make their living in the world, raise families and live anonymously within a secular society.

The priesthood of all believers, as the reformers called

it, means that every Christian stands before God as a representative of his or her neighbours and every Christian stands before the world as a representative of God. All Christians are part of that priesthood. They are ordained into it at their baptism. Just as Jesus accepted the role of servant in his baptism so each Christian accepts the servant role. That means an individual willingness to share with Christ and other Christians the burden of the world's pain. Praying, witnessing, caring are the shared responsibility of the whole Church.

Thirdly, there is the image of the covenant people called, like Israel, to a partnership in which God's redeeming grace is met by our obedience to his word. We are called to be God's covenant people, not in order to exclude others, but to be a sign to them of God's promises to all mankind. That love which is seen and witnessed to in the Church, is a love that will one day embrace all created things. The Church is the first fruits of God's salvific purposes as they are demonstrated in Jesus Christ.

On its side of the covenant, it lives in obedience to the commands of Christ as they have been recorded in the Gospels' account of his ministry. After centuries of caricaturing Jewish obedience to the Law, or Torah, Christians are coming to realise that they have much to learn from their religious kinsfolk. Perhaps the time has come to sit at the feet of Judaism and learn what it means not simply to believe, or to feel, but to do. The distinction between justification by faith and justification by works makes a valid theological point, but it outlives it usefulness where it weakens our resolve to *live* a Christian life. The Epistle of James is not, as Luther believed, an abberration, a denial of the supremacy of faith. It is a healthy reminder that faith and love have to be expressed in actions. Not vague actions that set out to love the whole human race at one and the same time, but actions that reach out to this particular human being, in this place, at this time.

In the parable of the Good Samaritan, Jesus taught

us the uncomfortable lesson that all the paraphernalia of religion are not worth a row of beans if we pass by another's need as if it did not exist.[1] As Rabbi Lionel Blue has said, the only religion that is real is that which we can get through the church or synagogue door. Just as Israel lives under the Torah, as given to Moses in the first covenant, so the Christian Church lives under the Torah of Christ in the second covenant. The ethical and spiritual demands of the second are no less than the first. Jesus told us that our righteousness is not to flag before that of the scribes and the Pharisees but to excel it.[2]

Body, priesthood, covenant people, these are only three of the images found in the New Testament. Common to all three is a recognition of the mutual dependency of each member of the Church upon others and the responsibility of each member for the health and work of the whole. The Church is itself on a journey towards human wholeness and maturity in Christ. It is not a static centre around which its members revolve like satellites. It is a pilgrim people. As such, it calls for the participation and mature commitment of its members if it is to function properly. In turn, it provides the ground of nurture and grace within which Christian men and women are able to grow.

In recent times, there have been encouraging signs that these images of maturity and responsibility have been taken ever more seriously by the Church. Yet, there remain times when the Church joins in the conspiracy of halted growth, as if it had a vested interest in immaturity. As in all good conspiracies, the work of undermining further progress is well concealed. There is no shortage of exhortations to grow, no limitations on nurturing, no reluctance to increase the vigilant oversight of shepherding. But it is a growth already determined by a rigid framework of expectations.

Efficient catechising which schools us in conformity with other people's ideas of God and how he acts, does not, and is not meant to, prepare us for that immensely risky business of responding to a God who lives more openly towards the future than we dare to believe is possible. We are nurtured on a diet of predigested food that spares us the necessity of chewing hard on anything we find difficult to swallow.

Our life in the Church is in danger of being forced down the same road into which our British universities are being compelled. It is an era in which Mr Gradgrind has astonishingly come into his own, in which 'facts' supersede all else in their importance. More and more, what we know becomes more important than how much we have thought about what we know. Reflection on the human condition, which has stood at the heart of the Western humanist tradition, is increasingly traded for knowledge that permits us to function in society in keeping with our people's expectations of what society is about. Learning becomes a process of fact and skill gathering, designed to shape us for our functional role. Little attention is paid to the contextualising of our knowledge within the wider horizons of past and future in which the present is only a fleeting moment.

Some forms of Christian education, likewise, are chiefly concerned with communicating facts and skills. They confine learning to the narrow parameters of one or other set of theological pre-suppositions. As if appalled by the freedom that was unleashed in the 1960s, they retreat into a conformity that reflects the managerial tidiness of contemporary society. Theology, it is reckoned, is safe only when academics, their work caricatured as hair splitting, limit their activities to university lecture rooms and see to it that their deliberations do not spill over into the lives of the faithful within the churches. As the Bishop of Woolwich was believed to pose a threat to Christian peace of mind in the 1960s so his episcopal brother in Durham is seen to threaten the equanimity of the Church in the 1980s. The questions raised by them, it has been argued, may be proper for the few but should be concealed from the many.

The Church, it is believed, must match the proliferating dogmatisms of our time with an even greater and better disciplined dogmatism. Truth is identified with dogmatism and dogmatism with certain indisputable facts. It is reckoned to be sufficient to know the facts. Theological reflection is considered a far more risky business. If the Church is to hold its place within a world riven by competing dogmatisms, then fact must be matched with fact, certainty with certainty, and creedal formula with creedal formula. The Church allows itself to be drawn into that magnetic field which will set it in polarity against all the other polarisations of our time.

Polarisation is believed to be the only way of establishing and maintaining identity. For we are witnesses of a strange paradox. In a time of great uncertainty, we retreat into certainties. We nervously eye the slumbering nuclear giant, we watch anxiously as the deserts advance and the areas of famine and poverty increase, we try to puzzle out the meaning of political struggles and the quest for national identities. The questions are vast and we resort to answers born of faction rather than the attempt to see things whole and thus to hold them in balance.

We narrow the world down to our vision of it. The terrorist inflicting pain seems incapable of feeling the pain of his victim whose flesh and blood is no more invulnerable than his own. Governments sustain their vision of the world by creating mythologies and coining vocabularies with which to explain them – 'evil empires', 'market forces', 'the national interest', 'democratic peoples' republics', 'liberation movements', 'capitalist imperialists'. In addition to having to unscrabble the language of mythology, we have to keep pace with the changing meaning of words. In the sixties, a 'radical' was someone who adopted an *outré* theological position and veered to the left politically. In the eighties, he is someone on the political right who advocates fiscal policies which will advance the already wealthy and enterprising individual.

The Church is in danger of responding to a perilous world in a way that will diminish the maturity of its members, not increase it. Faced with the heady mixture of rapid change and a resurgent fundamentalism in ancient religions and slightly less ancient political persuasions, the Church imbibes the potions of a grossly illiberal age. Some are prepared to accept this as the price of survival. It is, however, a far cry from that exposed and vulnerable figure who, on the cross, unshielded by a wall of invincible dogmas, unprotected by final certainties, died in the belief that love can survive only where survival does not matter, and resurrection can come only through the willingness to die.

Seeing things whole means seeing more than one opinion. It is a perspective that the Church is in as much danger of discouraging as the secular movements of our time. The Church can hardly avoid reflecting the spirit of the time within which it lives. It is never simply a mirror of contemporary secular movements, any more than the secular movements are simply mirror images of one another. Every institution and organisation brings its own pre-conceptions that mould and shape the wisdom of the day. Yet, neither can it avoid the cultural air that it is compelled to breathe. The development of the early Church cannot be explained without reference to the hierarchical structures of the Roman empire; the Reformation without a knowledge of the sixteenth century upheaval in the European nations; seventeenth century dissent without consideration of the parliamentary struggle and nineteenth century Church history without reference to the Enlightenment.

The air breathed by many who live in the late twentieth century is heavy with a conservatism that, unlike most of its historical antecedents, is not based upon consensus. It is largely indifferent to history, appealing to ahistorical myths and notions in order to reinforce cultural or religious identity. It is almost invariably combative and confrontational. It exists in Western democracies, in a declining minority within the Politburo, in Islam, in Judaism and in Christianity.

Within this inhospitable context, the Church has to teach its members the content and meaning of the Christian faith. That will mean coming to grips with the scriptural and historical core of what the Church believes. Experience-centred reflection which ignores that core of belief will be left without any enduring point of reference by which to gauge its truth. Learning, however, should be a process by which we grow. Its aim should not be to turn men and women into compliant pupils of one particular school of thought within the Church. The title of a recent book asks, *What Prevents Christian Adults From Learning?*[3] and suggests as one reason the need to be right and the avoidance of the pain involved in learning.

In the confrontational world of opposing ideologies, everyone wants to be right. Everyone also wants to be successful. The need to be right and the need to be successful create a formidable partnership when it moves into the business of expounding the Christian faith. Success and certainty provide men and women with an enviable identity within our contemporary culture.

The Church learns that success is to be found by instilling into its members a single-vision certainty. Christians are coralled into churches or massive gatherings of the like-minded where the vocabulary, the music and the dynamics of relationship provide security in an age of uncertainty. Sometimes forays are made into the problems of the contemporary world. There is even a hint of old-style political radicalism. Too often, however, it is tied to a theological fundamentalism with which it endeavours to make as much progress as can be made by an ill-assorted pair in a three-legged race.

Yet the Church is all that we have. It is that fair creature that, one day, will run in breathless adoration to meet the one who, from the beginning has loved her. If now, there are times when she is less than mindful of the maturity of her children, it is not for them to find maturity by forsaking her. Over the past twenty years, the flight from the Church into a proliferation of sects has proved to be no flight into freedom.

Sectarians who have shaken the dust off their feet, in the belief that the Church fails to measure up to the standards they believe to be appropriate, have fallen to the mistaken belief that they will produce something nearer to perfection. The history of the past five hundred years should teach us otherwise. The constant fragmentation of the Protestant reformation, carrying men and women ever further from the Church in which Luther was first nurtured in his Christian faith, has failed to produce communities more Christ-like, more committed to the task of theological reflection in the light of Scripture and the experience of the Church, or more loving in the service of others than the Church from which he originally separated. Catholic, Protestant and Sectarian alike, we comprise the same irritating mix of the godly and the ungodly, the zealous and the half-hearted, the radiantly good and the anonymously ordinary.

There are two approaches of our life in the Church that make it hard to accept this view of our corporate life. The first is our difficulty in handling dissent. The second, a belief that the Church should number only the converted or the committed according to any standard that we feel it right to impose.

The churches that find dissent most difficult to handle are those that themselves come from a tradition of dissent. They owe their very origin to a step taken by their fore-fathers away from a church of their own day. Dissent as a means of safe-guarding what one believes to be the truth is almost built into the self-understanding of those who

stand in a dissenting tradition. It forms part of their identity. Their origins tell them that truth is best served by
walking away from error. It is, unfortunately, a process
that has proved to be self-perpetuating. One step away
from error spawns a willingness to take another once error
is discerned in the dissenting group itself. In more struc-
tured churches, the temptation to schism is not so marked.
Aggrieved partners no long cohabit, but a common historic
loyalty remains intact, and charity and politeness, though
sometimes nearing breaking point, still manage to soften
the impact of conflict.

Where men and women have come to the Church looking
for certainties, dissent proves a disturbing experience.
Given the wider setting of our society in which dissent is
more and more unwelcome, its presence within the Church
meets with little tolerance. We grow more conformist. The
questions come to be feared as much as the answers. We
conspire to damn the questioner and silence his or her
answers.

Dissent, however, is essential for the health of any family
or group of people. Undoubtedly, it is possible to put up
a barrage of questions in order to evade any commitment
to truth. There is a dissent which is negative and destructive, a playing of academic games removed from the serious
realities of our Christian life within the world. It is not
always so, however.

Let us take one example. The doctrine of the virgin birth
has, in recent times, raised questions in the minds of some
people. Readers of the Gospels of Matthew and Luke are
hardly in a position to claim that the New Testament does
not teach the virgin birth of Christ. Indeed, the virgin birth
itself is not in dispute. Neither Matthew nor Luke, nor
anyone else in the New Testament, however, provide us
with a theology of the virgin birth.

Why was Jesus born of a virgin? The silence of the
evangelists has been more than compensated by the readiness of various Christian theologians to fill the gap. For

instance, it has been claimed that the virgin birth is a pre-condition of the sinlessness of Jesus. Does that mean that sin is transmitted through the process of human birth and, if so, at what point does it enter the process? Is it at conception? Does, as some have suggested, the act of inter-course itself plant the fateful seed and transmit the curse? Would Christ's perfect humanity have been impossible had it come from a solely a human source?

The questions appear largely academic until we examine their consequences for our understanding of our own human life. Is that union of man and woman in love of which the New Testament elsewhere speaks so eloquently, the source of all the world's ills? Is the first and best of women amongst us all to be honoured because, though a mother, yet she remained a virgin throughout her life, as the doctrine of Mary's perpetual virginity claims? Can Mary truly be the advocate and example of motherhood and virginity, achieving by grace what is humanly imposs-ible, namely being both mother and virgin? Is the ideal Christian, if Mary is such, someone whom by nature we can never be or someone, in her devotion to Christ and submission to God's will, we can all aspire to be? If Mary is a perpetual virgin and there was never any intercourse between her and Joseph, not simply before the birth of Jesus, but after, then can the Holy Family ever be under-stood as a family in the accepted sense of the word? Is it, in any way, a pattern for our untidy, joyous, affectionate experiences of family life?

The questions, far from being removed from our every-day concerns, affect amongst the most basic of our human activities. When we marry, when we make love, or when we choose celibacy, when we raise children, when we work through the business of being a family, we are doing things on which the doctrine of the virgin birth impinges. By implication, it seems to devalue these things. The ques-tioner may be persuaded that the virgin birth is what the New Testament teaches, but he or she has every right to ask the Church to come up with something better to explain it. There are surely finer things to be said of human love, of motherhood and of the family?

The Church cannot, on the one hand, encourage its members to grow and, at the same time, require them to be silent as they approach the Church's tradition. We cannot try to rehabilitate the human, too often despised within the Christian tradition and, at the same time, expect to perpetuate those aspects of the tradition that appear to demean and undervalue what is best in our humanity. Dissent may be disturbing. The citizens of Athens found it so when Socrates asked his questions, What is justice? What is a good state? We must not, as did they, ask our dissenters to drink a theological hemlock that will silence their questions and lay to rest their enquiring minds. The Church has either to look for better answers or, at least, better questions.

Dissent can be forestalled by defining more sharply those who belong to the Church. The heyday of Christendom provided the most generous definition. It was a net cast to include all those who had been baptised. In effect this meant the entire population, since infant baptism was a sign of incorporation into both church and nation. At the other extreme were the radical anabaptists. They believed that the Church should consist only of those able to make a conscious profession of faith in Christ. With the decline of the Christian tradition in the Western world, both approaches to Church membership have had to be modified. Within the Catholic tradition, the baptised still make up the number of the faithful. However, infant baptism is no longer a sign of nationhood. Where it is administered, it is in response to a conscious commitment to Christian beliefs and values on the part of parents, however tenuous and notional that commitment may be. Meanwhile, the ana-baptist mantle has fallen on the shoulders of the new restor-ationist churches that reject all main-line Christian

denominations and impose stringent standards of membership on those who wish to join them.

There is much that is admirable in both traditions. Both
sacramental integrity and zeal are desirable qualities in a
beleaguered Church. Neither, however, can fully
encompass the range of people's experience of God. Definitions of belonging, whether in terms of baptism or
commitment provide a necessary norm, a useful attempt
to describe as clearly as possible the heart of the Christian
experience. They cannot, however, be set down as parameters beyond which God is not to be found. Because
God cannot be contained within our words, because he
acts in freedom, because he is in dynamic relationship
with his world, he will always break the boundaries of our
definitions. This means that the Church will always be
ragged at its edges. Our Lord warned us often enough that
the Christian community is made up of wheat and tares,
or sheep and goats, and that it is God's task and not ours
to differentiate between the two.[4]

The Church is a community consisting of people at different stages of their pilgrimage. Those stages cannot be
accurately charted simply by reference to either sacramental or doctrinal norms. A complacent appeal to one's
baptism leaves unanswered the deeper questions of faith
and obedience to Christ. No good Catholic would deny
that. The new heirs of the evangelical tradition, however,
need to remember that reciting learned verbal definitions
does not shorten the road to maturity. To define oneself as
a Bible-believing, born again, spirit-filled Christian is to
do no more than state a definition. At our beginnings, we
do not yet know how much the Bible will ask of us, how
great the travail through which we will be born or how
long it will take the spirit to pierce the dark, unexplored
parts of our inner country.

Instead of deploring our raggedness and diversity, we
should glory in it. We are like Israel in her long march
from bondage to the promised land. There is a cloud that

guides us in the day and a pillar of fire that goes before us in the night. Some are closer to the cloud than others. Some see the light of the fire and feel its warmth. Others are a long way further back, seeing only the distant, flickering light playing at the edges of the night sky. Some follow their instincts, believing that this is the right route and that it leads to the promised land. Some have grown tired in the journey, but do not turn back, impelled by the hope of better things in the future. Some face each new day, eager to push forward, to cover more ground, hopefully to glimpse new landscapes. Others want the travelling to stop and to pitch their tents and stay where they are. And always there are those for whom Egypt and its securities have never lost their appeal. Some turn back, others try to recapture the security of their bondage and ensure the safety of their fellow pilgrims by fastening them in new fetters. Some have grown to love the desert. Others hate it.

The Church exists through an act of acceptance and forgiveness that God has made in Jesus Christ. Forgiveness and acceptance are not simply the door through which we enter, they are the milieu in which we live. It means nothing if our compassion is reserved for raw, new recruits and we have none to spare for our foot-weary companions. It is enough that we hold together, believing in the same God and walking in a similar direction. Like Chaucer's pilgrims, we all have our own story to tell. Our own experience will grow through listening to others. Acceptance of others is not a liberal fudging of the lines of demarcation. It is nothing less than a passionate avowal of God's ways with all of us.

Accepting our responsibilities as members of the body of Christ, living with dissent, and sharing our story with people greatly different from ourselves, are all ways in which the Church promotes our growth to maturity. It also does so by the provision of its resources.

The Church is a community that lives under the authority of the Scriptures and sustained by the spiritual grace of the sacraments. For the Protestant reformers, the 'marks' of the Church were the faithful preaching of the Word and the due administration of the sacraments. If nothing other than these were observed, there the Church was to be found. In word and sacrament we constantly discover how much God has given to us.

The Bible sets our personal pilgrimage within the context of God's leading of all his pilgrim people. From the garden of Eden with its infinite possibilities and its sense of terrible loss, to the city where all things are gathered together and restored in the New Jerusalem, the Bible traces the long and joyous journey. It is a journey never without hope. Even Adam and Eve as they look back to 'th' Eastern side . . . Of Paradise', so Milton imagined, set their faces to the future:

> Som natural tears they dropd, but wip'd them soon:
> The World was all before them, where to choose
> Thir place of rest, and Providence thir guide;
> They hand in hand with wandring steps and slow,
> Through Eden look their solitarie way.[5]

The Bible describes many journeys. Some where men and women have had to wipe away their tears and press on, believing that the world was all before them. There are journeys in which the path has risen to heights that we may never know and plunged into depths that we can only pray we will be spared. What cannot be shaken is the conviction that God is present in the heights and in the depths. Some, like Job, might feel that he is absent or silent, but this does not destroy their final conviction that he will speak to them. There is the unassailable assurance that they have providence as their guide.

The Bible is best understood when it is shared within the Church. Isolated from the ongoing story of a pilgrim people, it becomes a quarry for sectarian obsessions. We find it to be a guide in our own pilgrimage when we see the light it has thrown on other people's journeys. Within the preaching and testimonies of the Church we learn how other people have been influenced by the God revealed in the Bible.

This intermingling of Bible and community facilitates our progress in the faith. There is always the danger that we will settle for what we know and remain at the point at which we believe we have arrived. Alone, we can read Scripture in that way. We read it so as to confirm our present knowledge and to justify us in standing still. We do not see the distant hills towards which it beckons us. We are deaf to the compassion to which it calls us. In the Christian community, however, there will always be men and women who have travelled further and listened more intently to what the Scriptures have to say. They have sometimes seen the things to which we have been blind and listened to the truth to which we have been persistently deaf. Like Francis of Assisi, who has shown us what it means to take literally words whose sharpness we blunt. Like countless others, who see scriptural writ running through whole areas of life that we have yet truly to claim for God.

Alongside the Scriptures, there is the Eucharist. This is the pilgrim feast of the Church. It points back to where our journey began, in the sacrificial death of Christ upon the cross. It points forward to where it shall end, when Christ comes, either in the finally consummation of all things or, before that, in our own death.

The countless feet of generations of Christians have beat a path to the Lord's Table. They have come in the confidence that they will feed upon the Christ who is the unfailing bread of heaven. It is a sign of our pilgrimage that we hunger and thirst after righteousness. There is a longing within us that no palliative can satisfy. As Augustine said, there is a restlessness in the human heart that cannot cease until it finds its rest in God. It is a longing for grace, for forgiveness, for healing that will touch the very springs of our lives.

Christians vary in their expectations of the Eucharist. At one extreme, there are Catholics who believe that the substance of bread and wine become the very body and blood of Christ; at the other, the Salvation Army and the Quakers who believe that every meal is sacramental. Between them, a host of opinions hold some sort of central ground. The sign of the Church's unity, the Lord's Table has been the scene of debate and is still a place where people are divided by deeply held theological convictions. Controversy has led some to value it more and others to value it less.

Perhaps the divisions can be reduced to two simple, arguably over simple, approaches to the Eucharist. The first sees it as an observance, an act to be performed in obedience to Christ. It belongs to our obligation as Christians. Others see it as an obligation, but more than that it is a place of grace. Transcending what we do is what God gives. However the mystery of the divine presence is explained (and even the most devout Catholic would claim that it is a mystery that is explained), experience teaches us that here, in a way different to all other ways, Christ is given to us.

In terms of our growth to maturity, both approaches play their part. The Eucharist is an obligation in the sense that it is built into the structure of life. In the way that sleep, eating, keeping promises, showing a proper concern for those whose lives are bound to us in love, are all obligations. The Eucharist is not to be numbered amongst those activities that can be taken or left, used or disposed of. It does not depend upon the state of our feelings or the comfort of our circumstances. It belongs to life in the way that all that is most important to us belongs.

Obligation without expectancy can decline into legalism, however. Like loving duties performed long after love is absent. The Eucharist is a place of rendezvous with the Risen Christ. By the power of the word, the bread and wine become the mysterious agents of divine grace. We share again in the wealth of Christ's sacrifice, we take the life of the Risen Christ into the flesh, blood and bones of our humanity. The Eucharist is a gauge by which we measure Christ's ever deeper penetration of us and our penetration into him. The growing familiarity of the Eucharist, far from detracting from that deepening union with Christ, becomes an indispensable factor in it. It is a coming home. It is a growing recognition of the divine features. We trace him in the bread and wine. Its very familiarity and homeliness encourage us to look for him everywhere.

We need never go hungry again.

Notes

1   Luke 10.36–37.
2   Matthew 5.20.
3   John M. Hull *What Prevents Christian Adults From Learning?* (London: SCM Press 1988).
4   Matthew 13.24–30.
5   John Milton *Paradise Lost* Book XII (*Milton: Complete Poetry and Selected Prose* (London: Nonesuch Press 1948) p.349).

Chapter Four

Growth through Discipleship

To be called by Jesus is to be called to a life of discipleship. All the Gospels record the calling of the first disciples, the Twelve. The narrative makes them central to Jesus' purposes at that time, but there were others less in the limelight. For instance, there were the women, whose names are recorded, but whose role is largely concealed from us. The exceptions are Martha and Mary who have provided the historic Church with paradigms of active obedience and contemplative prayer. The glimpses we have of the women suggest that much more might have been written about them. We cannot overlook the fact that the first witness of the Resurrection was Mary of Magdala and that her response to the Risen Christ was *Rabboni* – Teacher.

The disciples do not seem always to have been clear about the purpose of their calling. The temptation to believe that Christ had conferred a new status on them, negotiable in worldly terms, seemed to dog their footsteps all the way to the upper room and the last supper. Christian triumphalism had its foot in the door from the beginning.

Aspirations after status, positions, power, the wrong sort of authority, met only with rebuke from Jesus. He at no time encouraged the disciples to imagine that this was what the kingdom of God was about. Maybe the heady combination of the words 'kingdom' and 'God' led them naturally in a hierarchical direction. The way they thought

about kingdoms and the way they thought about God were
parallel. The only models of kingdom that they had were
of national entities, sustained by political power and
governed by those nearest to the imperial throne.

When they moved from the earthly model to the divine,
the words power and kingship seemed properly to belong
as much to God as to any earthly ruler. Indeed, they swore
allegiance to one whose power reached far beyond the
limits of Caesar's empire, and whose kingship infinitely
transcended Caesar's kingship. Yet, too often, the nature
of God's power and kingship was indistinguishable in their
thinking from the nature of Caesar's. It took the cross to
demonstrate the extent to which our earthly notions of
power and kingship have to be reversed when we apply
them to God.

Likewise, models of authority could be transferred from
the secular to the religious. If power rested with those
closest to the Emperor, in religious terms it rested with
those closest to God.

This perception of discipleship persisted amongst the
Twelve and has never been wholly lost in the subsequent
story of the Church. And this in spite of the teaching of
Jesus to the contrary. For he told the Twelve and anyone
else who aspired to follow in his way that his kingdom was
about self-denial not self-assertion, it was characterised by
the willingness to carry a cross not the ambition to sit on
a throne, and that it existed to serve people not to intimi-
date them.

Behind our all too worldly vision of Christian status and
power lies our worldly view of God. He is that God of
whom we spoke earlier, the God of all our human pre-
suppositions of what God should be like. He is someone
other than the God whom we see revealed in Jesus Christ.
A God who clings to status is difficult to square with him
who 'made himself of no reputation' in Jesus.[1] A God who
controls by his power is not the God we see in Jesus,
limiting his power in order to make our freedom truly

possible. It is the God whom Jesus encouraged us to call 'Father' who calls us freely to subject ourselves to his will and to find in that subjection our true freedom. The signs of the kingdom are always countersigns to their worldly equivalents. We live by dying, we find ourselves by losing ourselves, we do not subject others to ourselves but serve them. In all this, we are one with Jesus who made possible his kingdom by his death upon the cross, who divested himself of divine glory to such an extent that he became unrecognisable except to a minority, and who knelt before his disciples and washed their feet.

If we believe that this is the essence of discipleship, then we will not be seduced into believing that there are other ways to maturity apart from the lifelong road of learning. The sons and daughters of the kingdom are not those who have undergone a cosmetic transformation of character. They are those who learn to empty their hearts that God's love might fill them; who bend their wills to the shape of God's will; who share God's passion and thus his suffering on behalf of the world. As Luther expressed it, in typically strong language, 'When Christ calls us he calls us to a bloody partnership'.

In the Judaism of which Jesus was a part, the rabbi was a respected teacher and interpreter of the law, the Torah. Recognising his authority, men would gather around the rabbi of their choosing and learn from him. Jesus, as he reminded them, was not chosen by the Twelve but had chosen them. He taught them his new and unique under-standing of the Torah. He opened up vistas of God that had not existed for them before, all summed up in the one description 'Father'. He told them parables that left something to their own imagination and required them to apply to their own lives the truth they had been shown in the lives of others. He took the trivial events of daily life, the weather, lost property, farm work, family disputes, and helped his hearers to see God within them.

Jesus taught and the disciples learned. His teaching was always ahead of them. It confused them by its very simplicity and the directness of its demands. He told a rich young ruler that he was to sell all that he possessed and give the proceeds to the poor if he was to find the kingdom.[2] Nothing could be more direct or unequivocal, but neither the rich young ruler nor those who have stood in his shoes since then have been able to embrace all the implications of such a simple injunction. Easier to believe that God spoke through Balaam's ass than to accept without question the command to sell and give to the poor, to turn the other cheek, to give your shirt to someone who has stolen your coat. Neither belief in the verbal inspiration of the Scriptures nor liberal openness to the social issues of our day embrace with enthusiasm such unrealistic demands.

Today, it is no easier than it ever was. But perhaps one credit point to be put down to the contemporary Church is that it does not evade the teaching of Christ. We no longer put the moral teaching of the gospels in scales where they are out-weighed by the rich Pauline teaching of grace. Grace and works belong together. Where the historic continuum of human experience has been ruptured by the unspeakable evils of the Holocaust, the Stalinist purges and the insanities of the Khmer Rouge, the pursuit of goodness is no longer seen as trying to lay arrogant claim upon God's free grace. It has become a terrible necessity in a world fed too long on a diet of misery and cruelty. Even if the teaching of Jesus be interpreted as an impossible standard set before us in some distant inaccessible future, nothing is lost by trying to reach out and touch it now. A hundred different sects and factions, religious and secular, testify that deeply held convictions and commitment to the point of martyrdom are not difficult to find in the contemporary world. It is goodness that eludes us. Its very scarcity seems to afford it instant recognition. The lone figure of Mother Theresa has to carry on her frail shoulders not only the poor of Calcutta but the aspirations after sheer goodness of millions of people.

It is through a world hungry for goodness that Jesus strides like the Christ of Pasolini's *Gospel According to St Matthew*. His words may be beyond us and his standards impossible of our attainment, but the longing is everything. As Jesus said, 'Blessed are those who hunger and thirst after righteousness, for they shall be filled'.[3] The spirit of this longing, this imperfect pursuit of an ideal, is embodied in the words of a Jewish rabbi who claimed that if one Sabbath were to be perfectly kept by all Jews then the Messiah would come. The fact that he has not yet come does not invalidate the centuries of observance and striving after perfection. The simple observance of the Torah, however imperfect, keeps alive the image and hope of the kingdom.

The teaching of Jesus both describes the sort of people we are to strive to become and prescribes the route we are to take in our striving. Both are necessary, the description and the prescription. The Torah of Jesus, like the Torah of Israel, exists to bring into being people who are whole and rounded and truly human. Jesus began the Sermon on the Mount not with his interpretations of the law or with ethical codes, but with the description of people.[4] These were the blessed ones. It is those who know their own poverty, who have not guarded themselves against sorrow, who are gentle, who long to see right prevail, who are merciful and pure in heart, who make peace and suffer persecution, it is these who show us what the kingdom is.

What Jesus describes is not so much an ordered piety as a generous humanity. We know it when we meet it. These are not the people who will be found guarding the world's concentration camps. They are not at the spearhead of the hatred that divides. They do not feed resentments, nor keep alive unforgiven ills and ancient quarrels. They do not cry out for us to recognise them, nor parade their virtue for our admiration. Above all, they do not make us feel that goodness is beyond our reach, since they embody in flesh and blood similar to ours the reality of the kingdom. They stand tall and they are remembered long after evil is forgotten.

A disciple is a person in a process of becoming. Paul described this process as growing to the full stature of Christ. It is a work of renewal that touches the roots of character, will and being itself. The chief agent of the work is the Holy Spirit who is given to us in our conversion and baptism. He represents the active and personal grace of God at work in the unseen depths of our lives. It is a work, however, that does not rest upon our passivity and compliance. We are not asked simply to let grace happen to us. The Holy Spirit, no less than God the Father, is to be understood in the light of the revelation in Jesus Christ. He is not a spiritual protoplasm, complex and colourless, that flows through us like alien stuff from another planet. He is personal. He comes in order that he might bring to our remembrance what Jesus said and did. He is given to us, but his coming into our lives requires our response and our active cooperation. If he is the chief agent of our growth into Christ, he also invites us into partnership. We are ourselves active participants in our own becoming.

This active response is elicited by Jesus in the second strand of his teaching, the prescriptive. Matthew portrays Jesus going to the mountain in order to give the new Torah of the kingdom. As Moses received the law at Mount Sinai, so Jesus stands on the mountain and spells out the new commandments.

We have already suggested that the teaching of Jesus sets before us ideals that are often beyond our reach. This does not mean, however, that its authoritative impact is in any way diminished. Jesus does not offer wholesome suggestions for the attainment of virtue. Just as the Ten Commandments, given on Sinai, were laws written indelibly into all human experience, so the commands of Jesus are to be received as the divine word for the present and coming kingdom. They are laws that have to be interpreted and re-interpreted by every new generation. Just as every new Jewish generation has to ask itself what the Torah means in this present time and this particular place, so Christians have to wrestle with the meaning of Jesus' teaching for their own situation.

The mass of Christians modify and adapt Christ's Torah. Those who take literally its commands stand out and are remembered. Francis of Assisi embraced poverty and disposed of all earthly possessions. At different times there have been those who have taken seriously the non-retaliatory ethic of Jesus and refused to take up arms or to resort to violence in the solution of national disputes. The pacifist position has always been part of the Christian witness, albeit that it has been held by a tiny minority. Whilst many churches will recognise the necessity of divorce where marriages have irretrievably broken down, those in the Catholic tradition take the teaching of Jesus on this matter as final and binding. Some have taken literally the command of Jesus to pluck out offending eyes or amputate transgressing hands, a shorter route to purity than inner wrestling with the lusts and desires of the flesh.

Those who choose poverty, non-violence or celibacy have always been the few. At times they have seemed eccentric, dangerous or naïve in the eyes of their contemporaries. Only a few have been persuaded to follow in their footsteps. Yet they have significance for all of us. It may be that we have to adapt or modify the teaching of Jesus. It may seem, at times, that love and humanity require us to act in ways that compromise the starkness of the teaching of Jesus. Given that it is so, the minority remain a sign to the many. For the ideal is indeed that we should value no earthly possession above the treasures of the kingdom, that we should seek a poverty of spirit that longs only for God, that we should refuse to retaliate and repay violence with violence, that we should accept marriage as a life-long commitment. The ideal is never disconnected from the real. Our compromises do not silence the word of Jesus nor lessen the bluntness of what he asks of us.

Though we earn our living and become involved in the financial hassles of house mortgage, family responsibilities and insurances, we can still strive after that inner poverty that discerns a true priority of values in our lives. It is possible to grow more generous, to be a good steward of our resources, to rejoice in the people we love and know that human life offers us nothing more valuable and, above all, to long for a deeper knowledge of the love for God himself. It is possible to refuse the way of violence and to break the spiral of blow and counter-blow, wound and counter-wound. It is possible to guard one's eyes from that lust which de-personalises those for whom our flesh may burn. It is possible to love those whom we marry to our life's end.

There will be times, many times perhaps, when we will falter and fall. But obedience to Christ is always lived out in an environment of grace. Command and forgiveness dwell side by side. Failure to rise to the high calling of Christ will be met with mercy. Mercy remains central to our experience of God. Yet that mercy does not nullify the command, it does not remove its obligation from us. The way to that character which Jesus describes as typical of the kingdom lies through the prescriptive teaching of Jesus. To be a disciple is to heed the Teacher. Our pilgrimage is one of moral as well as spiritual growth. The moral and ethical dimension cannot be isolated from that way, truth and life in which Jesus leads us.

The commands of Jesus were sometimes expressed with the directness of Torah and sometimes couched in the language of stories. The parables introduce another nuance in our understanding of Jesus' teaching. The teaching of Jesus, any more than any other law, cannot be mechanically applied to human situations. The need for interpretation is always present. The God we see in Jesus does not remove responsibility from our shoulders nor deny the role of imagination in our pursuit of goodness. Both responsibility and imagination are necessary if we are to be creative in our moral and ethical response to the Torah of Christ.

The parables tell us just how much is left to our creativity. In the parable of the Good Samaritan, we have to transcribe into our own times the roles of priest, Levite, Samaritan and wounded Jew. The conflict between Jew and Samaritan is remote from our own historical experience so we are left to draw our own parallels. It is an exercise in which the Church has not always been successful. Too many of history's wounded Jews have learned that they could expect more mercy from a passing Samaritan than a passing Christian.

There will always be situations in which there is no clear, explicit word, only a parable for our minds to wrestle with and apply. So, in the teaching of Jesus, there is both the explicit and the open. Obedience and creativity are held in tension. The parables remind us that the teaching of Christ has to be earthed in the untidy world of human affairs. They are stories that illustrate ways in which the commandments of Jesus are to become a part of our own story. To be faithful to Jesus, our obedience must be stimulated by our imagination, it is a matter of moral and spiritual artistry as much as conformity.

Obedience and imagination are both factors in our response to authority. Living the Christian lie is far more than doing what we are told. It is envisaging the kingdom of God in the world and taking risks in making its coming possible.

There is, implicit within the teaching of Jesus, a massive authority. It was this that his contemporaries recognised, some responding gratefully, others angered and threatened by what seemed to undermine their own authority. For us, the authority of Jesus is communicated indirectly through the Bible and the Church and directly through our present experience of the Holy Spirit. Christians will vary in the importance they attribute to each of these factors.

Our basic authority is the Bible, since this is the first and unique witness to the deeds and sayings of Jesus. This means that our moral and ethical life has to be based on reflection of Holy Scripture, the sort of reflection that we associate with meditation and prayer. We have seen that a theoretical assent to the doctrine of verbal inerrancy by no means leads to a consistent application of the harder sayings of Jesus in personal life. Faced with demands which are quite exceptional in their rigour and which fly in the face of what we see as acceptable self-interest, we all compromise what we read. We compensate by being uncompromising in our advocacy of those aspects of Jesus' teaching with which we have come to terms and which we have been more successful in translating into a way of life. So we may be more biblically consistent in our sexual relationships than in our duties to the poor. Or we may be more enthusiastic in our commitment to the zealous sword that divides than to the peace-making that reconciles.

For some Christians, the authority of the Bible is bolstered by the authority of the Church. There is authoritative Church teaching on chastity, the sanctity of marriage, divorce and homosexuality. Our duties to the poor, however, are more often the subject of exhortation than legislation, whilst issues of justice, non-violence and freedom are assigned to the grey area of politics which Christians either shun or explore with varying degrees of enthusiasm. Quite rightly, there is no comprehensive source of authority, based either on the infallibility of the Scriptures or of the Church, that will ensure our commitment to the full range of our Lord's teaching.

The external authority of the Bible and the selective authority of the Church has to be set against the inner submission of the believer to Christ in prayer and openness to the spirit. The path to maturity does not lie through enthusiasm for biblical infallibility or unquestioning submission to the Church. The first is a theory that may or may not touch the springs of our daily living, the second an abdication from personal responsibility. In prayer, we open ourselves to the whole gamut of Christ's teaching. We seek the Holy Spirit's guidance and inspiration. It is this inner acceptance of Christ's authority, this personal assent which involves heart, mind and will, that lies at the heart of our growth and formation in Christian character. Bible and Church are indispensable to our growth in Christ since, apart from them, we cannot know the word of Christ, nor the ways in which Christians have interpreted it. They remain external to the formation of Christian character, however, unless we inwardly submit to Christ. As with discipline, that only is effective which we willingly impose upon ourselves.

In prayer, we are open to the searching of the Scriptures and the Holy Spirit. The word in its fullness enflames, inspires, judges, guides, warns, encourages and lures us. There are ethical precepts that have already been incorporated into our life-style and with which experience has made us familiar. There are others to which our wills have not yet been brought into submission. Constant reflection on the parables of our Lord will make us more aware of the ethical decisions that we have yet to make. There are standards that Jesus has set before us to which we have not yet given our consent. The parable is a story, a drama in which we have to learn to cast our own lives. It provides a key to our own story, and a way of placing ourselves in the unfolding story of Christ's work within the world. It reminds us that obedience is creative and risky.

Our Lord himself reminded us that all spiritual and ethical imperatives are gathered up in the one commandment, that we should love one another. This was the New Commandment. In the Gospel of John it is the *only* commandment, given to the disciples at the Last Supper, as the New Covenant was about to be initiated.[5] It is a commandment that embodies both the descriptive and the prescriptive aspects of our Lord's teaching. It describes what we are to become and prescribes the means of our becoming. We are to be people motivated by love and subject to love's claims in our lives.

Love, however, is a word that deceives by its very simplicity. In English, the broadness of its application makes definition difficult. As a verb, it has many uses. I love my wife and children. I love Paris. I love pasta. I love long, summer days. I love God and God loves me. We deplore the fact that one small word has to achieve so much. A little knowledge of Greek reveals to us that the Greeks were at an advantage. They had four words, memorably explored, in our own time, by C. S. Lewis.[6] There was affection (*storge*), friendship (*philia*), sexual love (*eros*) and the love of God (*agape*). For the last, Lewis uses the Latin *caritas* (charity). Of the four loves, it is *agape* that is most honoured by Christians. This is love as it is revealed in Jesus, that unique, divine, selfless love that does everything that is necessary for our salvation, regardless of the cost. The theologian Anders Nygren tried to demonstrate its supremacy by comparing *eros* and *agape*, describing the first as essentially self-gratifying and the second as selfless.[7] This facility for finding the right word for the right occasion, it would seem, helps us to avoid confusion. God, kith and kin, Paris, pasta and summer delights do not have to be lumped in one unseemly mass with one thing in common, that we love them all.

Yet the very untidiness of the English usage of the word love is not without its virtues. In our daily experience, different sorts of love do not live in monadic isolation from one another. Even St Paul managed to confuse *eros* and *agape*. Writing to the Ephesians, he compares the love that a man should bear to his wife to the love that Christ has for his church.[8] In his words, *agape* provides the example for *eros*, but *eros* also becomes a means of understanding *agape*. Contrary to Nygren's definition of *eros*, sexual love has been the motivation for utterly selfless and courageous actions. However successful we may be in placing love in different categories, each spills over and invades the territory of the others. Human affection can be touched by divine concern and friendship be marked by selflessness. And even sexual desire, as Abelard learned from the love that Heloise bore him, can be a means of understanding the cross more profoundly.

Above all, the many ways in which the English language uses the word love reflects the universal setting of Christian love. Though its origin is in God, it yet embraces all our loving. Indeed, all love, of whatever quality and however far removed from the divine ideal, has its origin in God himself. Even that love that John Betjeman glimpsed across a Bath tea-room, as a man and a woman held hands

> She, such a very ordinary little woman
>   He, such a thumping crook;
> But both, for a moment, little lower than the angels
>   In the teashop's ingle-nook.[9]

When we isolate *agape* from all other loves, we provide an excuse for those forms of Christian love that seem to make us less, rather than more, human. Fellowship lacks the commitment of friendship, and Christian love the passion of sexual love. *Agape* is not a form of love that exists alongside other forms, it is an added dimension that transforms all our loving. What *agape* provides is a basis for our loving and a focus in its expression.

The base upon which love rests is God's love to us in Jesus Christ. It is his love that awakens love within us and which continues to fuel our love in order to keep it alive. It also has to find a base within ourselves, however. Here, our normal use of the word love can be misleading. Invariably, we use it to describe a state which engages our feelings, it involves our affections. We use it of things we like. We may place it at any point along a scale of intensity, but always it is associated with warmth. It describes our feelings for certain people, for our favourite places or food, for our pleasantest experiences. Love is associated with feeling good, whether it be about people or Mozart's music.

The root of Christian love is not in the affections, however. It is in the will. Christian love is the will to act towards people and created things in a Christ-like way. It involves decision and choice. It requires us to behave in a certain way. Our feelings are not always visible and cannot always be accurately perceived by those around us. They elude observation. The will, however, has to live a much more public life. The consequences of our choices are seen in our actions. We may take our Lord's parable of the sheep and the goats as an example. People cannot see how we feel about those who are hungry, or thirsty, are strangers or naked, sick or in prison. Our wills, however, do not enjoy such anonymity. What we *do* about the hungry, the thirsty, the stranger, the naked, the sick, the prisoner, is open to observation. We do something or we do nothing. We act wisely or unwisely. We respond or we remain locked in our private worlds. Our feelings allow us to luxuriate in noble intentions. The will provides no such escape.

Our Lord, especially as his words are recorded in the Gospel of St John, often talked of his own ministry in terms of compliance with God's will.[10] Union with God is more than a mystical experience, however strong the feelings of joy and awe that may result from it. God does not so absorb us into himself that we have all responsibility taken from our shoulders. Loving union with God requires us to make loving decisions in our day to day life. We cannot escape choices about what we do. The God I have been trying to describe, does not force his will on us. Rather, he reveals it and then invites us to accept it as our own. It is in that acceptance that we discover the grace of the Holy Spirit. It is by the exercise of our will that we accept God's

will in our lives, but it is only by the grace of the Holy
Spirit that we can do God's will.

There has always been a difficult paradox at the heart
of Christian discipleship. Christ's call to deny ourselves, to
take up the cross and to follow him, involves a conscious
consent on our part. It requires a decision that calls upon
all our resources of faith and courage. Yet, when we have
thrown everything into our commitment, we realise that
we are utterly dependent not upon our resources, but upon
the grace of God. The firmer our resolve to seek God's will
and to do it, the more reliant we become on grace. As St
Augustine succinctly put it in a prayer, 'Lord, command
what Thou dost give; and give what Thou dost command'.
The grace of the Holy Spirit does not diminish our personal
responsibility; on the other hand, the exercise of that
responsibility in compliance with God's will is possible
only through the grace mediated to us in the Holy Spirit.

Dependence upon the Holy Spirit also reminds us that
we live within the mercy of God. We learn that our wills
are notoriously unreliable. We do not always do the good
that we will to do. The will may find the spirit slothful and
the body a reluctant partner. In such moments, we turn not
to a lessening of the will's demands, but to the assurance of
God's forgiveness. Living by grace is living under mercy.

Love resides in the will. That effectively pins it down. Our
wills are always under greater constraints than our feelings.
The country of our affections has movable borders, there
is almost infinite room for expansion and diminution. The
will has to work within tighter parameters. It deals with
the present and the particular.

Love may begin with a vision of the universal. The
Christian Gospel proclaims a universal love: 'God loved
the world so much that he gave his only Son, that everyone
who has faith in him may not die but have eternal life'.[11]
That is the breath-taking vision of love to which the Gospel

introduces us and in which it invites us to share. It places no one beyond the reach of love. None has been excommunicated in advance; the kingdom precludes no one. It is that setting within which our lives are lived. It discourages us from drawing circles which include some and leave others out in the cold. There are circles that we draw and within which we live, such as the circle of the family or of the Church. We need those circles as places where we help to establish our identity and to which we turn for sanctuary. We must not imagine, however, that God draws the circle where we do. His circle embraces all created things and all live within the sphere of his providencial love.

Humility compels us to recognise, however, that only God can sustain a love like that. We cannot carry the whole world: we have to be part of the world that God carries. In this the will comes to our aid. In our visions, in our dreams and in our prayers, we may love and embrace the world. Our actions, of necessity, have to opt for most modest aims. Again the parable of the sheep and the goats helps us to focus our loving. At one level, the level of the general and universal, we can say that Christ loves the hungry, the thirsty, the stranger, the naked, the sick and the prisoner. Indeed, he is found in them. They fill the world. They are everywhere. But if love is to be effective then it must come down to another level, from the universal to the particular. In terms of our wills, there are only these hungry and thirsty people for whom I give, in the spirit of Christ's generosity, from the resources that Christ has given me. There is only this stranger, awkward, defensive, tentative, whom I try to make welcome and at home. There is only this sick person by whose bed I sit and whose feelings I try to share. There is only this person in prison whom I visit if I can, but to whom, if he or she is in some distant labour camp or prison, I write letters and pray for.

The saints, in spite of all their potential for vision and inspiration, insisted on the minute particular as the place where love is active. In his work *Self-Abandonment to the*

Divine Providence, Jean-Pierre de Caussade reflected on what his translator Kitty Muggeridge calls 'The sacrament of the present moment'.

> It is not by considering what you are doing elsewhere that I shall become what you wish me to. It is by accepting your presence in everything . . . It is only because we fail to take full advantage of divine action that we turn to so many alternatives. Such diversity cannot give us what we find in that singleness of purpose from which we derive the power to do great things.[12]

Few are remembered more for this emphasis than St Thérèse of Lisieux. Her Little Way was an invitation to all Christians to turn the realities of the present moment into the means of serving and loving God. As one of her biographers described it, she 'democratised holiness'. She saw the opportunity for love within the reach of everyone. Confined as she was by the restrictions of a nineteenth century *petite-bourgeois* Catholic family or, later, the severity of the Lisieux Carmel, she loved the people around her and made the details of a singularly anonymous life the means of glorifying God . . .

> Sometimes, when I read spiritual treatises, in which perfection is shown with a thousand obstacles in the way and a host of illusions round about it, my poor little mind grows very soon weary, I close the learned book, which leaves my head muddled and my heart parched, and I take the Holy Scripture. Then all seems luminous, a single word opens up infinite horizons to my soul, perfection seems easy; I see that it is enough to realise one's own nothingness, and give oneself wholly, like a child, into the arms of the good God.[13]

In the twentieth century, the need to choose actions, at once the most human and the most God-like, was never more difficult than for the Jews who suffered in the extermination camps. Viktor E. Frankl describes his own experience of those choices.

> We who lived in the concentration camps can remember the men who walked through the huts comforting others, giving away their last crust of bread. They may have been few in number, but they offer sufficient proof that everything can be taken from a man but one thing: the last of human freedoms – to choose one's attitude in any given set of circumstances, to choose one's own way. And there were always choices to make. Every day, every hour, offered the opportunity to make a decision, a decision which determined whether or not you would become the plaything of circumstances, renouncing freedom and dignity to become moulded into the form of the typical inmate.[14]

The limitations of the Carmel or the unspeakable horror of the camps are not the setting of most of our lives. But if men and women can make choices favouring humanity and holiness in such settings, we can expect to do no less in the place where God puts us. We cannot go back to the past to demonstrate what love means. We can only be grateful for its good memories and ask forgiveness for its sins. We cannot reach out into the future and dream of what we intend to do, like Peter promising a faithfulness unto death.[15] We cannot be transported to other situations or crave more congenial opportunities. We have only this moment. We have only these people whom our hand can reach out and touch. We have only this place, whether its horizon reaches as far as the eye can see or no further than three paces and six heartbeats. It is here, nowhere else, that we deny ourselves, take up the cross and follow Jesus. And it is here, as everywhere else, that he fills with his grace.

Notes

1 John 15.16.
2 Luke 18.22.
3 Matthew 5.6.
4 Matthew 5.1–16.
5 John 13.14.
6 C.S. Lewis *The Four Loves* (London: Fontana 1963).
7 Anders Nygren *Agape and Eros*.
8 Ephesians 5.22–33.
9 John Betjeman 'In a Bath Teashop' *Collected Poems* p.129.
10 John 5.17,19,30.
11 John 3.16.
12 Jean Pierre de Caussade *The Sacrament of the Present Hour* (Trans. Kitty Muggeridge (London: Collins 1981) pp. 90–91).
13 Ed. F. J. Sheed *The Collected Letters of Saint Thérèse of Lisieux* (London: Sheed and Ward 1949) p. 292.
14 Quoted in *The Blue Guide to the Here and Hereafter* (Eds Lionel Blue and Jonathan Magenet (London: Collins 1988) p. 95).
15 Luke 22.33.

Chapter Five

Growth through Human Relationships

When asked what was the greatest commandment, our Lord replied, 'Love the Lord your God with all your heart, will all your soul, with all your mind'. That is the greatest commandment. It comes first. The second is like it: 'Love your neighbour as yourself'. Everything in the Law and the prophets hangs on these two commandments.[1] With those words, Jesus set our lives within a cruciform pattern of relationships. Like the cross itself, reaching into heaven and embracing the world, we live in a vertical and horizontal pattern of relationship. We are in relationship with God and with one another.

If we place these two relationships in the shape of the cross, then we realise that they are inseparable. There is not a religious world in which we relate to God, and a secular world in which we relate to others. There is not a communion of the spirit with God and a messier set of relationships, based on kinship, friendship, or sex, between ourselves and others. Our relationship to God and that which we have with others, intersect. They hold together and belong to each other.

The New Testament, in various ways, highlights their mutual dependence. The request for God's forgiveness in the Lord's Prayer is linked with the forgiveness we are to give to others – 'Forgive us our trespasses, as we forgive those that trespass against us'.[2] In his first letter, John tells us that there can be no question of loving a God whom we cannot see whilst hating a brother or sister whom we can.[3] The two are a contradiction, they cannot be isolated from each other.

The central relationship of our lives is that which we have with God. It belongs to the core of our being where we know ourselves loved, accepted and forgiven. It is irrigated by the constant stream of grace which God pours into our lives through the Holy Spirit. It is nurtured by the Scriptures and the Eucharist where, in the truth and the life that lie deeper than words, or bread and wine, Christ mediates himself to us. It is the hunger in the midst of fullness that drives us to our prayers and makes us willing to wait for the deeper knowledge, the more immediate awareness of divine love. It is the goal of our pilgrimage.

From this central relationship we derive our understanding of all our other relationships. That is why we need to recognise their interconnectedness. The ways in which we believe God relates to us and we relate to him, profoundly affect the way we relate to others. It might be argued, of course, that they are two different ways of knowing and of relating.

Our relationship with God includes features that are not characteristic of our relationship with other people. The one is between the divine and the human, the other between human and human. Our ways of knowing God depend upon analogy and image: our words, our doctrines, even the way in which we describe our present experience of God, are all at one remove from the reality itself. Humans are quite different, we argue. We all share a common experience and, even when words elude us, we know what it is that we share.

Further, in our approach to God, there is awe and mystery, even fear (as long as we understand what we mean by that forbidding word). We worship God. We kneel before him. In love and gratitude, we obey him. Such experiences are not part of the interaction between human beings. That being so, how can we draw analogies from the one central relationship to all other relationships? Is it not inevitable that we will relate differently to God from the way in which we relate to other people?

It is not necessary to empty of divinity, awe and mystery the one experience, to see in it parallels with the other. Even the 'otherness' of God is a parallel with the 'otherness' of people. The act of loving God teaches us something about the act of loving people. In loving God we do not turn him into an image of ourselves, we do not confuse his identity with ours or ours with his. We cannot fit him into a framework within which he measures up to our expectations or conforms to our predictions. To know God is to be aware of his freedom and, deriving from that, to be more acutely aware of the freedom that he has given to us. We can never own God. We do not possess him. His very 'otherness' imposes a detachment which is essential if we are to know him as he is and not end up worshipping a projection of our own fantasies.

Most of what I have said could be equally true of the way we should relate to people. There is in human beings an 'otherness', a core of being that is personal, hidden and probably never completely known by another human being. Nor are people images of ourselves. They are not the vehicles of our ambitions, they do not exist to serve our purposes. They, too, have freedom and we have to live with the consequences of their decisions just as they have to live with consequences of ours. Above all, we never own people. That is an insight that does not come naturally to us. There is an inner drive to possess what we love, to make love itself a form of possession. But, as St John of the Cross reminds us, true detachment is not indifference to others, nor resistance against loving them, it is the refusal to possess them. Only through that refusal can we truly know them and truly love them.

There are features of our relationship with God, however, which can maim or destroy our human relationships if not properly understood. We have already looked at the concept of God's omnipotence and the way in which it distorts our image of him if it is not seen in the light of the cross. If we see God's relationship to us in terms of his power, then we see one who determines our actions: the more we are filled with his Spirit, the more we are controlled by his will. To see it in this way is to empty it of those characteristics of partnership and consent that are so basic to our Lord's revelation of God the Father. To see any relationship, even that which we have with God, in terms of the control of one by the other is to diminish the essential nature of our humanity. God creates us as free beings and limits the consequences of that freedom neither in the way we relate to him nor to one another. God lives with it, just as we have to live with each others' freedom.

When we refuse to acknowledge the role of freedom in our relationship with God we endanger its role in human relationships. If God is valued chiefly for his power, then we shall come to value power for ourselves. If God's power is seen in terms of his control of us then we legitimise our desire to control other people. We create a world of hierarchies in which it becomes important to know where we stand in the pecking order. By whom are we controlled and whom do we control? We fall into the same trap as the disciples on their way to upper room, arguing about who shall be greatest in the kingdom of heaven. Like them, we are confused and embarrassed by the figure who kneels before us, girded with a towel, and washing our feet.

Sometimes we are placed in positions of authority where the issue of power is unavoidable. Authority thrusts power into our hands and we are held accountable for our stewardship of it. It is significant that the larger part of our experience of such authority lies within the Church and the family, communities that have proved their capacity for either enriching people beyond measure or devastating them.

Authority within the Church is unavoidable. A community called to tasks so diverse relies upon men and women who will accept responsibilities and leadership, together with the authority that goes with them. The temptation for kingdom-building is never far away. Control of the church budget, the church fabric, the flower-arranging committee, the uniformed organisations, the Sunday school or any of the other multifarious activities of the church can unleash in us all the symptoms of unregenerate ambition. More sinister are the pressures towards conformity and success that are placed on the ordained ministry. Temptations to take short-cuts are temptations to abuse power. We practise forms of conversion by control, creating environments in which heightened emotion is wedded to intellectual passivity. We attack the legitimacy of people's ordinary experience, the experience they share with countless other human beings, and offer the prospect of a supercharged spirituality that will ride above the vulnerability and ambiguity of the truly human. We identify our opinions with the will of God and thereby disarm those who think differently or have heard differently in their prayers and reading of the Scriptures.

The way of the cross is far more risky. It invests our authority with the only legitimate form of power, the power to love. All power within the Church should be exercised in order to enhance people's freedom, not to diminish it. One of the exercises of that freedom will be our subjection to one another and to Christ. But it will be a subjection based upon trust, not blind obedience or fear. Within the Christian community we will come to recognise people who have climbed higher in their prayers than have we, have understood the Scriptures and the Christian tradition in ways that we have scarcely begun to understand them, have passed through harsh human experiences and, by the grace of God, emerged stronger and more charitable. It is because we recognise in them the authentically Christian and human, that we are willing to be subject to that auth-

ority with which life and experience of God have invested
them. It is even possible to subject ourselves to those who
are young in their authority, as long as we recognise in
them an openness to the experience of the whole
community.

The Church is a place where we are learning together
and growing together. It is more likely to achieve that ideal
if it recognises the magnanimity of the God in whom we
are neither Jew nor Gentile, slave nor free, male nor female,
but one new humanity in Jesus Christ. In other words,
Christ has delivered us from racial models of power and
preference, he has demolished an order in which anyone
can rightfully be the possession of another, and he has
begun a revolution in our understandings of sexuality and
the mutuality of men and women that it is taking us a long
time to understand.

The second sphere within which we experience authority
is the family. It is here that the revolution in our perceptions of the relationship of male and female are most
felt. It is also a revolution that brings us eyeball to eyeball
with certain passages in the New Testament.

In Colossians 3.18–25 and Ephesians 5.21–6.9 advice is
given on the way Christians are to conduct themselves
within the relationships of husband to wife, parents to
children, and masters to slaves. The second passage, with
its emphasis on mutuality of duties and its recognition that
we are to be subject to one another and all of us subject
to Christ, softens the blunter teaching of the first. We are
still faced, however, with the difficulty of reconciling much
that both passages contain with our twentieth-century perceptions of human relationships and the sort of doctrine of
God that we have been exploring in these pages.

Perhaps we will be encouraged to take a bolder approach
to the teaching on family relationships if we begin with the
question of relationships between slaves and masters. The
hermeneutics of the New Testament's implicit acceptance
of the institution of slavery are well known. The apostles

lived at a time when slavery was basic to the Roman economy and enforced by Roman power. Any questioning of that system, any fostering of discontent, any incitement to rebellion would have met with a swift and bloody response from the Romans. The slave rebellion under Spartacus in 77BC could leave no one in any doubt as to Roman reactions to any attempt to undermine the institution of slavery. The Church could only take a few steps towards the ultimate dismantling of the system by insisting on a new relationship between slaves and masters within its own fellowship. They were to share an equal status in Christ and to drink from a common cup in his Eucharist. Other than that, the Church accepted the institution and reflected on how people were to live within it.

In the twentieth century our views would be very different. Slavery is wicked and abhorrent. Improving the lot of slaves, making more humane the relationship of master and slave, reminding masters of the authority of Christ beneath which they stand, does nothing to alter the evil of the institution itself. At this point, the teaching of the New Testament can be translated into the twentieth century only by the most liberal interpretation of its original meaning and a thorough recognition of the development of Christian perception in the intervening two thousand years. Our white brethren and sisters in South Africa are not to be counselled to make *apartheid* more humane, and our black brethren and sisters to accept their subjection as in the Lord. *Apartheid* is evil and calls for a Christian commitment to its abolition not its modification.

On the issue of slavery, few contemporary Christians would find it difficult to read the New Testament in the light of history and through twentieth-century spectacles. The same would not be true in their perception of the family. Indeed, in some of the new sects, astonishingly, the belief in the submission of women has taken on a new lease of life, and the rod has found its way back to the mantelpiece as an instrument of parental discipline. There have been times when some Christians have argued that slavery belongs to the natural ordering of creation itself. Enthusiastic defenders of that argument would now be difficult to find. The same difficulty would *not* be encountered in finding those prepared to defend an order of creation in which women are to be subject to men and the family viewed as a hierarchical and patriarchal institution. The teaching of the Colossian and Ephesian passages, for instance, would be used to support that view. Slaves might lose their chains, but women remain bound by nature and tradition in natural submission to men.

We find ourselves on more congenial New Testament ground if we focus on the role of women in the ministry of Jesus. By her reception of the incarnate Word into her womb, the Virgin Mary stands first amongst the faithful. She is the first Christian. Martha and Mary are figures that have illuminated our understanding of prayer throughout the Christian centuries. The women who kept vigil at the cross, who remained true to the Sabbath observance on that fateful Easter Eve and performed the last loving rites over the body of Jesus, are forerunners of the countless women who have kept alive the faith of the Church in dark times. It was a woman, Mary Magdalen, who was the first to be entrusted with the apostolic role of witness and herald of the Risen Christ. It is women such as these who make us realise that the complementary roles of men and women are not best served by the submission of the one to the other.

Those who oppose the changing role of women within society and the family, stress the necessity of observing the different functions, characteristics and roles of men and women. To advocate equality and partnership, however, is not to deny difference. Our changing perceptions of human relationships enhance the difference between men and women and make it a source of greater enrichment to both. The Mary who gave birth to Jesus was also the singer of the song of freedom. Her Magnificat celebrates the liberation of all humanity and the reversal of the world's power structures. It would be ironic if the only power structure exempt from the redeeming work of Christ were that which has traditionally institutionalised the ascendancy of men over women. Mary of Bethany has rightly been the inspiration of all who embark upon the lonely path of contemplative prayer, whilst Martha, her sister, affirms for us, over the tomb of Lazarus, the final power of the resurrection to transform all things. Again, it is the Easter greeting of Magdalen that echoes across the centuries, 'I have seen the Lord!'

All this has wider implications for the Church and for society, but it is within the family, within the most intimate and loving of relationships, that men and women can grow to realise that they exist for each others' freedom and growth in Christ. The Ephesian passage provides a growing point that takes us beyond some of its own assumptions. If wives are counselled to be subject to their husbands, husbands are also counselled to love their wives as Christ loves the Church. Understanding the nature of that love will do more than anything to undermine the old hierarchies. For Christ's love is demonstrated in the call to partnership, in a profound desire that we should grow to wholeness and maturity. It is a love that is reciprocal, our love for him and his love for us, answering each other like the intermingling voices of a two-part fugue which draws in the other voices of humanity for its completion. Such is the love that exists between man and woman in marriage. It is a love based upon partnership; a love in which each covets the growth of the others' life in Christ; a love that provides an ikon of God's wooing, loving and faithfulness to the whole human race.

If power is eschewed in our understanding of the relationship of husband to wife, it has also to be handled with caution in our understanding of the relationship of parents to children. An extraordinary trust is placed in the hands of parents as they accept the responsibility of their children in the first, fledgling years of their lives. The intimacy and secrecy of family life provide opportunity for the sort of abuse to which our society grows increasingly accustomed and from which it can never cease to recoil. Jesus did not place the child at the bottom of the hierarchical pile, the final recipient of the chain of command. He placed a child in the midst of grown people and told them that this same child pointed the way into the kingdom.

When the Church lost its roots in Judaism, the experience of children within the family was impoverished. In Judaism, the family is the place of human and spiritual growth. In the common life of the family, the faith is celebrated and interpreted. It is the youngest member of the family who asks the meaning of Passover at every *Haggadah* meal. On Sabbath eve, the cups of celebration are drunk, candles lit, and children blessed. At its best, family life is a mingling of faith and humanity. It is a place that protects us within its loving structures, but which also provides a nest from which to fly into the freedom of the wider world.

The structures that we create within the life of the family are inevitably forms of power. The creation of those structures lies largely in the hands of husband and wife. If they are based upon the pattern of God's dealings with us, then they will be designed not to produce children who are clones of their parents, but free individuals who will not be afraid to love, to think or to question. Where the parents are successful, they will awaken in children such trust in the ultimate goodness of all things as will enable them to live in the acceptance of their responsibilities towards others and in the confidence of those who are at home with their own heart and mind.

Human relationships provide the scene for some of our greatest failures in life. Our more public achievements, whether in career or personal attainments, cast a long

shadow within which are concealed our private
shortcomings.

In Western society, the family is still enormously important and valued by the majority of people. Yet statistics tell
their own sad story of failure. Many marriages end in
divorce. Some end quickly. Others fall apart, in a mysterious and hurtful way, after years of loving, sharing and
child-raising. A wife or husband, bewildered and wounded,
stares at the gaping hole left at the centre of his or her life
by the infidelity of a partner. Sometimes there is no adult-
ery, no betrayal, simply the desire to end the marriage and
go separate ways.

Families, too, may disintegrate. Parents and children
are driven apart, finding themselves on either side of a
generation gap. Children become caught up in a sub-
culture, sedulously propagated by different forms of media
and rigorously imposed by the pressures of the peer group.
Parents and children may come to feel that although living
in the same house, they are living in different cultures,
using a different language and a different set of values.

It is not necessary to fly to such extremes, however, to
experience a sense of failure. We remember that we have
been less than loyal to our friends, less than attentive to
the channels of communication upon which friendship is
dependent, too absorbed in our own affairs. We recall our
failures within our marriages. We have been impatient,
cold, unpredictable in our moods, selfish in our demands.

We do not always understand our children, nor they us.
When we have done what we believed to be right, humane
and tolerant, the relationship hoped for does not materialise and, within the strange network of family relationships,
we become and remain strangers.

The Bible is a stranger to none of this. It does not
quarantine us in our human failures, surrounding us by
the high wall of its own perfect patterns of relationships.
On the contrary, our experience is mirrored in its pages.
At times, it describes a passion and bloody-mindedness of

which we may wish to plead innocent. Of the first two brothers in the biblical narrative, Cain murdered his brother Abel. Jacob unwisely spoilt his son Joseph and caused resentment and envy amongst Joseph's brothers. The friendship of David and Jonathan marred the relationship between Jonathan and his father, Saul. David seduced Bathsheba, having cruelly betrayed her husband. Hosea was deserted by his wife, Gomer. There is even that *contre-temps*, that clash of duty and loyalty, between the twelve-year-old Jesus and his parents when they took him to Jerusalem for his first Passover. In the ministry of Jesus, there are collisions between the disciples, arguments between brothers over their inheritance, and the story of a wayward son, a distraught father and an envious brother.

What the Bible and our experience testify to is that human relationships can be lived only in grace. Fundamental to them is the constant need to be forgiven and to forgive. The phrase in the Lord's Prayer that deals with relationships is all about forgiveness, inseparably joining together the need to be forgiven and to forgive: 'Forgive us our trespasses, as we forgive those who trespass against us'.

Forgiveness lies at the heart of the Christian gospel, that message which the Church is called to proclaim and with which it is identified. Without forgiveness, human beings are impelled into a downward spiral of pain in which the wrongs we do one another are followed by reproach and retaliation, gathering momentum as wrong begets wrong. Caught in that whirlpool, we are buffeted and violently thrown against others. There is neither time nor space for these wounds to heal. Without forgiveness, we spin from one circle of violence into the next.

Forgiveness liberates us from the circular sequence of wrong, reproach, retaliation and new wrongs. When we are forgiven and forgive, we break the sequence, we hear and speak the word of grace and acceptance that prevents the perpetuation of old sins and the creation of new ones.

We create the space in which old wounds can heal and we can touch one another in blessing instead of being jostled in bruising confrontation. We escape the whirlpool and our lives flow on into broader streams, carried into new surroundings, freed for new possibilities.

The God who comes to us in Jesus Christ comes in forgiveness. In the cross, all the images of forgiveness are present. Through Christ's sufferings we are healed. In Christ, the Father reconciles us to himself. At the cross, the dividing walls of enmity are broken down, the mortal enemies of the human soul are vanquished. Through the cross and resurrection, we are set free. We are raised to a new life in which neither sin nor death have dominion over us. The language of the New Testament is alive with hope, and new beginnings, the breaking of harsh, inflexible moulds, the disruption of the destructive circle of sin and retaliation.

Yet our attempts to explain Christ's work of atonement have sometimes left us with a view of God that can be as crippling to our human relationships as the absence of forgiveness. Just as a certain emphasis on the power of God can veil a very human desire to control and dominate, so there are ways of looking at forgiveness that can be equally manipulative.

Christian theology sometimes brings us face to face with a God who operates on a system of rewards and punishments. The need to punish even finds its way into the central affirmation of free grace and forgiveness, since forgiveness is made possible through the punishment of the Son in our place. This way of looking at the atonement has never lost any of its attraction. Here we see a transaction taking place. Here there is some rationale, some reason, for our forgiveness. We deserve to be punished, but Christ has accepted punishment on our behalf. Therefore, by accepting this, it is possible for us to be forgiven and to escape punishment. When we look at the atonement in that way, we can see what is going on.

But it raises problems. Theological problems arise first. How can any change in a situation be effected by transferring guilt from one to another? Guilt is never transferable. Love can never make us guilty with someone else's guilt. Punishing the innocent in place of the guilty changes nothing. Further, forgiveness has been granted only because punishment has been accorded and accepted. We are forgiven because the books have been squared, the debts have been paid, there is nothing outstanding. It might be argued that, under such circumstances, forgiveness becomes a formality like the cancelling of an invoice that someone else has paid. Is that forgiveness? Is that really the new word, unlike any other word, that deals not with punishment and retribution but with the breaking of the whole relentless circle of sin and retaliation? For punishment, too, is a form of retaliation.

To reject this interpretation of the atonement is not to deny that Christ stands in our place. Indeed, his solidarity with us is the key to our understanding of his work on our behalf. He is made one with us and receives into his own soul and body the onslaught of sin. At the cross, he is drawn into the whirlpool that swirls down into the midst of hell itself and in it speaks the saving word of forgiveness. He comes to stand in solidarity with our death that we might be drawn into solidarity with his Resurrection. He brings us forgiveness in the very act of accepting our flesh and blood as his own. In the end, forgiveness cannot be bought, nor earned, nor justified. It is given, freely. That is the meaning of grace.

The reason for this detour into atonement theology may not have been immediately apparent, but now we see that all our ways of thinking about God impinge on our relationship to the world and to one another.

Forgiveness offered in the terms I have just described is a forgiveness that is placed in a punitive setting. It does nothing to remove the need to punish. It compels us as Christians to hold in fine balance both the offer of free forgiveness and the necessity of punishing sin. It confronts us with a punitive God who will send thunderbolts on those judged heretics, appalling diseases on those straying from an acceptable pattern of sexual relationships and, as many still persistently believe, illness upon those who sin. It reinforces that punitive bias which has manifested itself in Christianity in phenomena such as the Inquisition, on the Catholic side, and moral judgmentalism on the Protestant.

Within that framework, forgiveness in our personal lives becomes anything but unconditional. It is hedged in by an array of requirements which have to be satisfied before it can be offered. Where pain has been inflicted upon us we, like God, wish to inflict pain in return before applying the balm of forgiveness. There is our need to see the books balanced. We want the offender to suffer the same pain as we have; not simply to see the hell in which we have been, but to inhabit it as well. We want the suppliants for our forgiveness to 'eat humble pie'. It is not enough that the prodigal come back from the far country, he must come with his tail between his legs and must listen to a catalogue of the woes and sorrows of which he has been the cause. The fatted calf and the celebrations can wait for the more pressing business of compensation for the lost years.

It will be argued that forgiveness has to take place in some sort of moral context and that it can never be painless. That is true. If we do not recognise that we live in a personal environment which is dependent upon the mercy we show to one another, if we are blind to the pain that we cause others, if the forgiver and the forgiven never shed tears together, then forgiveness is a sham. There is a fundamental longing for justice in all of us, but seen in purely punitive terms that longing is diverted not satisfied. Justice is the revelation of the clear truth of the situation within which we all live. The Last Judgement will reveal the cruelties and inhumanities that human beings have inflicted upon one another, and we will either then accept that life is possible only through the grace of forgiving or being forgiven or we will die eternally.

Justice is possible only because there is forgiveness. In our relationship with others, forgiveness is not something offered once we believe that the appropriate punishment has been meted out, in whatever form. Forgiveness is the first and most urgent response to the wrong that has been done to us. Justice, the healing of the relationship, the putting right of the attitudes, the cruelties, the sinful thoughtlessness that first gave birth to the sin, may then flow from the forgiveness offered and received.

Where we show forgiveness we discover that there is no contradiction, no tension, between love and justice. Both forgiveness and justice are the work of love. Above all things, in the very core of his being, God is love. We are called to be like him. If we are swift to respond in our forgiveness, then the lengthier work of justice becomes possible. We have created a setting within which relationships can be repaired and restored. Those who had been torn apart can grow more closely together. The wronged wife or husband, the wilful child, the blundering parent, whoever we are, mercy gives us the opportunity to begin again. Forgiveness diverts the downward, circular thrust of the whirlpool and carries us out into streams of living water where there is opportunity to find one another again and to restore what had been destroyed.

It is a sign of our progress in Christ, the more we realise that we live by mercy. At the outset of our journey, we do not fully know the hurt of which we are capable. As we look back, we see the foolish and the loveless things that we do, even to those who are closest to us. The foolish things we can, with time, forget. Foolishness is part of our raw immaturity, our slowness in growing wise. It is not so easy to forgive the lovelessness: the thoughtless insensitivity to a friend, the selfish exploitation of the love of our spouse, our gruesome adolescent contempt for our parents and our blundering decisions in the lives of our own children.

Without forgiveness, these are the burdens that will only grow heavier the further time carries us away from the sins we have committed. It is as we look into our own heart that we may feel that we deserve only punishment and God's rejection. We know that our salvation has come, not through the settling of scores with a punitive God, but through the one word that could give us life, the word of forgiveness. God makes possible not simply the miracle of his acceptance of us but also the miracle of our own acceptance of ourselves.

That is, perhaps, where all our forgiveness has to begin. If we reject ourselves, we will reject others. If we indelibly mark our own sins on our conscience, we will just as indelibly mark the sins of others. If we cannot believe that God has accepted us, freely, lovingly, in utter grace, then we will be unable to accept others. Once we know all these things, however, we are then liberated in order to forgive. It is not a knowledge that will come all in a moment, even in a moment of sudden conversion. But as it sinks into the deepest places of our knowing, in our hearts, in our perceiving of ourselves and of others, then we will grow more magnanimous, more generous.

Our way with others will always be determined by what we see to be God's way with us.

Notes

1   Matthew 22.36–40.
2   Matthew 6.12.
3   1 John 4.20.

Chapter Six

Growth in the Life of the World

Up to this point, we have seen our journey in terms of an environment familiar to Christians. We began with doctrine and went on to prayer, church and discipleship. With human relationships, we moved into an area of life which we share with everyone else. The world of faith has its own pre-suppositions, its own language, its own way of viewing life. Our human relationships involve us in the messier aspects of human life. Here we have to share the world's language and face predicaments similar to those faced by our neighbours.

The sphere of our relationships brings us face to face with that vast landscape which lies beyond the safer confines of the Church. Christians have invariably spoken of it as 'the world'.

We can speak of God loving the world, but not of Christians loving the world. Indeed, to accuse a Christian of loving the world too much is another way of describing him or her as being guilty of compromise and half-heartedness. 'Worldliness' is a sin. Bunyan's 'Worldly Wiseman' was foolish in things of the spirit.

This attitude to the world has been a characteristic of various attitudes and movements within the Christian Church.

In the third century, a number of Christian men and women left the cities of the Mediterranean world and made for the desert. They chose places that were rugged, inhospitable and deserted. They were compelled by a search for God and desire to escape from the sights and sounds of the city, which proved a distraction to the life of the spirit. With the conversion of Constantine early in the fourth century, the flight to the deserts gathered momentum. People, no longer able to make the offering of 'red martyrdom' at the stake, in the arena, or on the wheel, chose the 'white martyrdom' of self-denial and deprivation.

Repelled by the growing comfort and conformity of a Church that had become the official religion of the Roman empire, they sought something that they believed to be nearer to the heart of the Gospel. From the status-seeking, the currying of favours, a church that they believed had grown effete, they sought the solitariness of the desert. Here, they struggled to attain a condition of utter simplicity in which Christ was to be central to all things. They fled from the lure of possessions and of sex. Here they owned nothing and schooled themselves in a detachment, called *apatheia*, which left them free of natural human desires.

This urge to escape from the world has always been present in Christianity. It has produced the monastic communities and, with them, men and women of enormous spiritual depth and grace. Ironically, they have also been communities that have had a marked influence on the life of the world on which they have turned their back.

It is not the monasteries and convents alone that have nurtured this spirit of world renunciation. It has been part of the discipline of the Church. A suspicion of the material world has too often lurked amongst Christian beliefs. If, at the theological level, there has been a lively awareness of the dangers of dualism, of sundering matter from spirit, the human from the divine, at the level of day-to-day perceptions of the world and the way it is lived in, things material and essentially human have been viewed with misgiving. The world has always been regarded by the Church with some alarm. There have been times when it has been able to integrate sexuality and human happiness into Christian practice only with the greatest difficulty.

The 'gathered churches' of the reformation and onwards, withdrew from a wider church that they believed had grown 'worldly' and from a world that they believed to be ungodly. The lines of demarcation were drawn boldly, sharply separating those who belonged to Christ and the Church from those who belonged to the world.

This sense of separation has been heightened by viewing the world as the realm of 'the lost'. Beyond the borders of the Church has lain a territory inhabited by those whose ultimate destiny is to be damned. Human beings and their cultures, whatever their qualities or virtues, whatever the constraints under which they live or the disadvantages by which they are dogged, whatever the handicaps they bring into the world or are thrust upon them in the course of their lives, are lumped into a vast mass which none can measure nor number and assigned for perdition.

The world itself sends confused signals. There are aspects of human behaviour that seem fit only for the most dire and eternal of punishments. In the whole realm of creation no other species of being can match the cruelty displayed by humans to their own kind. People inflict unspeakable pain upon one another. In the concentration camps of this century, they have hounded to their death millions, who were cursed, denied human identity, beaten, starved, gassed, gunned down. States oppress and persecute their own citizens. Terrorists murder indiscriminately in causes that will be resolved either by reconciliation or not at all. Nearer home, human beings cheat one another, rob one another, are indifferent to one another's needs, vie with one another for status, and despise one another on grounds of race or creed. Males behave in ways that seem capable of understanding only to the behavioural psychologist, channelling aggression into tribalism, raping women, beating their wives and abusing their children. The awful litany of human wickedness shouts at us from our newspapers and holds us mesmerised before our television sets.

And yet there are other signals from the world. Pop stars harness the idealism of the young and raise millions of pounds for the relief of the needy. Wherever there is injustice, there are innumerable brave men and women who struggle for a more humane society and sacrifice themselves in great and good causes. They speak out passionately against all forms of mass destruction. They revere the earth and fight to protect it. They protest against the bloody slaughter of the whale and carefully assist a threatened species of tiny bird to survive. They write words that do not die but articulate the aspirations of one generation after another. They write and make music, and from the disciplined partnership of the symphony orchestra to the artistry and dexterity of the concert pianist, they create an aura of sound that hints at worlds beyond this one.

They fall in love and find great joy in the sight, touch and presence of those they love. They form friendships that last as long as life itself. They marry and find within the devotion of their shared life a profound happiness. They bear children whom they surround with the security of love.

They suffer pain bravely and compassionately respond to the suffering of others. They build hospitals for the sick and hospices for the dying. They patiently encourage the mentally retarded child towards a wholeness of life. Disabled people do not surrender in the face of their disabilities, but wheel themselves to glory in marathons, and make blindness a way of seeing.

This, too, is the world. The awful things do not spill over and contaminate the whole, making everything corrupt and worthless. If there is enough evidence to confirm the Christian conviction that the world is evil and a barrier to holiness, there is alternative evidence to prove that goodness flourishes and that the image of God is not totally erased from the features of humankind. Our sin and the repugnance that we feel at its fall-out is expressed in the Christian doctrine of the Fall and original sin. This teaches us that there is a fatal flaw, or bias, in us all, and that every part of our life is touched or threatened by the sin that is within us. It is a condition that compels us to turn to God as our saviour. On the other hand, we continue to live in a world that is the work of God and sustained by his providence.

If we are to live with ourselves and in fellowship with other people, then we need to believe in and affirm the redeeming work of God in Jesus Christ. We are held by grace, and it is grace alone that opens the way to fellowship with God, that makes possible the forgiveness which enables us to live with ourselves and to forgive and be forgiven by others. By the side of that, however, we need to believe in and affirm the doctrine of creation.

All things that are come from God and have their being in him. Theologians in the Middle Ages sometimes speculated about the sort of world that God might have made, had he not made this one. It was believed that there was an infinite number of options from which God might have chosen. The greatest amongst them, Thomas Aquinas, believed that the world in which we live reflected and bore evidence of the God who had created it. The world, he said, provided countless analogies, models, by which we might know God. Just as Jesus had told us to look at human fatherhood to understand something of God's fatherhood, so Aquinas urged us to look at the world and, through it, to begin to know God.

This carries profound implications. If the world is an ikon of God, then it derives from his nature. In other words, we should not speculate on other possibilities that might have been open to God, but dare to believe that, if he was to create, this is the world he would have created and none other. If, as Cardinal Newman asserted, we have to live with the awful consequences of 'some vast aboriginal calamity', namely the Fall, we also inhabit a world that continues to bear the imprint of God's creative hand on men and women who, however disfigured, have been created in his image.

When we emphasise human wickedness and see the world as a realm in which Christians have no proper place, we deny the Lordship of the creator whose presence penetrates every part of the created order. When we ignore human wickedness and try too quickly to forget the moral outrages we perpetrate against one another, then again we deny the Lordship of the creator and the moral framework within which he has set our lives. We have, on the one hand, to refuse to be intimidated by evil and not accept it as the only data upon which we build our picture of the world in which we live. We inhabit the world as the sons and daughters of the creator Father, seeing in a wayside anemone a glory greater than Solomon's and, in an act of alien charity from a Samaritan to a Jew, evidence of a goodness that reflects the nature of the God who made both Samaritan and Jew. Yet, on the other hand, we must never underestimate the power of evil, either in ourselves or in the complex arena of human affairs. With Julian of Norwich we can assert both that 'Sin is necessary' but also that 'all shall be well, and all shall be well, and all manner of things shall be well'.[1]

Our Lord perfectly expresses, as he perfectly expresses all else, the relationship between redemption and creation. He came to redeem by entering into utter solidarity with the world which the Father had created through him. In Jesus, we believe that God has perfectly revealed himself in the form of our humanity and in the sphere of our human life. There could not have been a more perfect identification with humanity, reaching as it did into the very darkness of death itself. As Christians, we draw universal conclusions from that one act of solidarity. The Incarnation has significance for the whole human race. The sphere of God's redeeming activity *is* the human and *is* the world. He brings into being the Church not for its own sake, but for the world's sake.

Living in the world involves living openly to the culture of which we are a part. That does not mean living uncritically. There are aspects of our culture which are mindless and manipulative, especially when cultural fashions can gain such widespread access to people's homes and listening space through mass media. There are forms of culture that keep people locked up in xenophobic attitudes to people of other races, that limit the growth of people's vocabulary and that create a mood of passive acquiescence instead of creative participation.

Christian growth involves the skills of discernment. Whilst recognising what is worthless, we will also recognise what is good in and of itself. We are not required to come to terms with our culture by building a half-way house in which we can live comfortably. We do not, alongside the secular cinema, try to set up something that we call 'Christian' cinema, or match theatre with 'Christian' theatre or, once the airwaves have been opened to the dubious competition of market forces, seek to saturate them with 'Christian' television. We can end up with something far more sanitised but no less manipulative than its secular counterparts.

When we seek to create special Christian forms of art or culture then we should do so because we have something specifically Christian to say. We should not imagine, however, that we have created something better or of more lasting value than that created by other men and women from the richness of their human experience. Nor should we feel it necessary to create Christian forms because our Christian lives are set against a different backcloth or portray a different scenario. We live in the same world as other people and have to run the same gamut of emotions. Within our culture there are writers, film-makers, artists, journalists, comedians, architects, politicians, law makers, who see the world true and reflect it accurately in what they do.

Being a Christian requires neither the manufacture of home-made substitutes nor a little more than grudging recognition of men and women who analyse our human condition with almost surgical accuracy, or who turn our contemporary values upside down in their humour, or can write plays with the power to move us to tears. Because we live in solidarity with other human beings, we will recognise that we learn about ourselves from our culture as do other people. Schaeffer's *Amadeus* is not a 'Christian' play, but no Christian can fail to be moved to questions and, in the process, to a greater understanding of the God in whom we believe. A jazzband has no explicit message to communicate. It makes music, it picks it out of the air. It is a celebration of great virtuosity and musical inventiveness. There is nothing to prevent Christians joining other members of the human race, enjoying the music for itself and sharing its exuberance.

May I be forgiven a personal recollection? In the church of my youth, it was customary to hear 'testimonies'. People would give anecdotal accounts of their lives and, without embarrassment, tell others of the ways in which God had been present. I remember one young woman who came to visit our church. She sang a song, piously commendable in its sentiments but banal and indifferent in its music. Somehow, her voice utterly transcended its inferior quality. It was a glorious soprano, rich and tender, that took the entire chapel in its embrace. Afterwards, in her testimony, she told of her earlier training and her ambition to become an opera singer, all of which she had abandoned on her conversion in order to sing for God's glory. Instinctively, something within me rebelled and argued that God could not require such sacrifices. This was a voice that deserved something better than Sankey. I knew little of opera then, but now as I listen to the aria 'Più docile io sono' in *The*

Marriage of Figaro in which Mozart glimpses a forgiveness that, in his music, seems to come straight from heaven, I remember that voice in my youth. Opera could never have been a foreign environment for such a voice, nor singing Mozart an unworthy pursuit.

Living in the world also requires us to believe in the loving justice of God. Culture is not morally indifferent. The good and the lasting have to live side by side with the worthless and, at times, the evil. It is said that there were guards in Auschwitz who, off duty, listened to the music of Beethoven. This juxtaposition of hell and sublimity does not involve us in the rejection of Beethoven. It does, however, compel us to recognise that even the finest expressions of human creativity may be unable to transform human beings. We do not necessarily change the world by civilising it.

The persistent presence of evil in the world has sometimes encouraged Christians to retreat from it and leave it to its own devices. The world in its wickedness, it has been affirmed, stands under the judgement of God and, on the Last Day, will be called to account. This scenario is both true and less than true. It is true insofar as it recognises that the final resolution of all things lies in the hands of God. It is less than true when it draws the conclusion that Christians are consequently to abdicate from their responsibilities within the life of the world. Justice does not have to wait for the end of the world.

Part of our problem is that we portray justice in negative and punitive terms. Justice, as we often describe it, is the punishment that God will finally mete out on a wicked world. It is about penalties and retribution. It is administered to a human race in which everyone from accountants to assassins, pimps to loving fathers, nurses to Mata Haris, murderers to market gardeners, are lumped together and condemned. Justice is to be feared.

When we make justice a fearful thing we undermine the foundations of any good society. What would be truly terrifying would be the belief that there is no justice in the world neither now, nor at the Last Day. Were there no justice, there would be no separation of good and evil, no assurance that evil will not so ooze into the very nature of things that it will survive into an endless eternity. The presence of God's justice, responding to the evil in things now, and passing judgement upon them at the end, is the cause for hope, not fear. In a world where unspeakably cruel things are done, justice is to be welcomed.

It is to be welcomed in our own lives. Justice brings the truth about ourselves, it discloses the darkness concealed within us. Without that shining light, however bright and painful it may be, we remain half-healed, not fully at one with ourselves. We need justice to tell us who we are and what it is that needs forgiving in our lives. That is not a punitive work, it is a work of grace. If we are to be changed from glory into glory, then the layers of self-deception and unacknowledged sins have to be peeled away so that we might truly be God's beloved.

If we live with justice in our own lives, then we can live with it in the world. Faced with evil, we are not to run away but to affirm the justice of God which is sovereign over all things. For many Christians that literally means standing with the oppressed, feeding the hungry, speaking out against tyranny even though doing so may cost them their freedom or their lives. Love and justice fuse into one and often require a sacrifice that is nothing less than everything.

Not all Christians, by any means, live at those frontiers where grace and oppression collide. We all contribute to that climate of belief, however, which insists that justice, in God's name and by God's grace, is to be done in our human affairs. Because we are not at the sharp end of the cosmic conflict between good and evil, we do not shrug our shoulders and walk away, leaving these things to those who are. Turning points in the human story, moments of great significance, are formed from a thousand small decisions and made possible by a *milieu* of belief, and trust and prayer. Justice is forgotten only when ordinary men and women, by their silence, by their acquiescence, allow it to be forgotten.

Living in the world requires us to live openly towards the experience of others. Most modern societies are multicultural and multi-racial. Though some may make a last-ditch stand, fewer and fewer are bound together by a single set of cultural values, a single understanding of religious experience or even a single language. This faces Christians with a dilemma. They believe in the excellence of their own convictions. They also believe those convictions have a unique claim on every human being. Christianity is a universal religion which regards no part of the world, no other culture or religion, as 'off limits' to its mission.

There are those Christians who believe that the proper approach to people of other faiths, and of none, is always one of mission and evangelism. There are others who would emphasise dialogue. The two are not of necessity mutually exclusive. A concern for mission is not necessarily the prerogative of those who see no virtue in listening to others. Neither is a willingness to listen a denial of one's belief that what Christ has done, he has done for the whole human race.

The wider issue of Christian attitudes to people of other faiths, however, is only the backcloth against which most of us have to live our lives. The real business of relating to other people can be reduced to small, immediate situations involving a relatively small cast of players. Each has a history that has made him the person he is. Other people's stories and the way their values have been formed give shape to their joys or create irrational fears. But their stories are no less significant than our own. Our beliefs are not a package that we have carried intact throughout our lives, they are a living part of ourselves, strengthened by our experiences, tempered in the questions that life has addressed to us and, sometimes, washed in our tears.

Beliefs are not abstractions for other people, any more than they are for ourselves. A Jew carries within him the long historical memory of his people's suffering, sometimes his own painful experience of antiSemitism; the Moslem has grown in the fasting of Ramadan and formed his convictions out of the words of the Koran. But for every one of these people who cherish religious beliefs there are many others who have no clear, articulate faith to which a recognisable label can be attached. These, too, have their stories which are as much tales of spiritual struggle, questions, joy, pain and growing perception as our own.

Surrounded by this diversity, we may be tempted to believe that he is heard who shouts loudest. Or we may be dissuaded from the path of dialogue by the warning that those who do take it run the risks associated with relativism. Relativism, however, is a fact of life. Everything is relative to something else and cannot be fully understood without reference to it. Christianity cannot be fully understood, except in its relationship to Judaism. People's half-digested beliefs or non-creedal values have to be related to communities in which they have lived and the ways in which they have heard and perceived the faith of others.

Listening does not imply that we agree with everything that we hear. Nor does it require us to be silent about our own story. Listening is essential, nevertheless, if we are to understand the people around us and not see them as exactly fitting our prejudices and conforming to our presuppositions. It would be easier, perhaps, to retreat into the church where people speak 'our' language, conform to 'our' values, or reinforce our view of the world. But the incarnation of our Lord provides no such model of retreat. He was in the world, amongst people, and he knew their stories.

He knew Nathaneal's scepticism. He knew the marital problems of the Samaritan woman at the well. He listened to people's pleas for help and healing. Being a Christian does not involve staking out our ground in the midst of the world and then building a fence around it. On the contrary, we are to take the fences down, to remove the 'middle wall of partition,'[2] to build bridges across the gulfs that divide people. But we can only do that if we are prepared to listen.

Lastly, *living in the world means celebrating earthly things.* The creator portrayed in the opening chapters of Genesis is not a God engaged in a reluctant task. As aeon succeeds aeon and the world grows into ever more rich and varied life, God looks upon what he has made and sees that it is good. When man and woman have been created, then he rests. Sabbath becomes a rejoicing in the world, God's satisfaction, his enjoyment of the high mountains, his delight in the dazzling, darting fish that swarm through the seas. God regards all that he has made and is happy.

That same happiness in creation characterised the ministry of Jesus. He saw the signs of the Kingdom in the splendour of the natural order and in the rich variety of people's lives. Towards the end, he took bread and wine and made them signs of the divine love towards us. He gave them to us that we, too, might celebrate. Not indifferent to the world's pain, but knowing that its brokenness has been healed, pain become the source of wholeness and death the means of life.

None of us is part of the world's permanence. We are born, and most of us in the Western world are welcomed by a boundless generosity in all things. We pass through, and leave the imprint of our decisions upon the world's face. Then we leave, and other generations inherit the ever-increasing legacy of good and ill. It is a journey in which, as we shall see, we should have a proper sense of our own transience and a vision of the City of God which awaits us beyond this created order. But it is a journey during which we are not to close our eyes, nor shut our ears, nor dispense with our sense of smell. Rather, we should share God's happiness in the world.

The Christian faith will always contain elements of the

supernatural. The possession of the supernatural, however, is never the consuming passion of the Christian. We must not make the mistake of believing that the world is only validated by the extraordinary and miraculous. The supernatural is that which reveals God's providential love where effect cannot be traced to cause. It breaks in upon us in ways that are unrehearsed and above and beyond God's covenanted gift of daily bread. Yet its purpose is not to turn the created order and the commonplaces of our humanity to drabness.

The extraordinary exists to draw from the ordinary its light, its colour and its life. The miraculous moment assures us of the validity of everything we touch and handle in our daily lives. The Apostle John was at pains to tell his readers that the truth that he shared with them was that which 'we have heard; we have seen with our own eyes; we have looked upon and felt with our own hands.'[3] The incarnation of Christ draws our eyes to the world, to the fully human, and tells us there, in the great mystery of it all, to see God.

We are not meant to create our own religious world, side by side with the world that everyone else inhabits. The only way of being alive is not simply belonging to a *live* church. Sundays are not beacons in a desolate landscape nor Christians saints in a sea of sinners. The whole world is alive. It is ringed with music. We belong to it and our flesh and blood will not allow us to separate ourselves from it. Whether we choose to be or not, whether we accept it with gladness or not, we are bound in solidarity with all creation and, by that same bond, we are bound to Christ.

Christians in the Eastern church believe that whenever the Holy Eucharist is celebrated the whole earth is renewed. So we, when we gaze at Christ's wounds in broken bread, and see his blood cleansing the world in outpoured wine, celebrate a death and resurrection that has made all things new. In the sacrament, the bread, the wine, the water; in daily life, the touch of another's hand, the grit of men and women who stare pain in the face, the good earth, each blade of grass and opening flower, in all these signs, 'religious' and 'secular', we see God's footsteps.

When we leave the world, we shall not need to ask God's forgiveness for our tears. For, though we go to a glory that now we know only in part, we are not ashamed to acknowledge that we have loved this place of our pilgrimage. It is no slight upon the God who awaits us since, after all, we knew him here, found him here, and here learned to call him Father.

Notes

1 Julian of Norwich *Showings* Chapter 27 p. 225.
2 Ephesians 2.14.
3 1 John 1.1.

Chapter Seven

Growth through Suffering

The enigma of evil in a good world comes home to us most sharply when we encounter suffering. Suffering is the most common and widely shared consequence of living in a world that is at odds with itself, a place in need of healing and renewal.

Christianity, with its central symbol of the cross is, it would seem, preoccupied with pain. The cross or crucifix is the focal point for our eyes in many places of worship. They are drawn towards the gaunt, twisted figure who seems to hang forever in great pain. This is not pain as most of us experience it. The hideous succession of cruelties in the story of Christ's death are remote from our own experience. We do not see men, their backs lacerated by the scourge, or stumbling beneath the weight of the cross, or nailed to it by their hands and feet. In the world today, of course, far too many people are not strangers to that sort of pain. Indeed, it is refined by the use of modern technology and the additional horror of mental torture.

The cross, however, is valued as a symbol not simply for what it says about pain but for everything else that it signifies. The cross is the womb from which life has come, it is the strong fabric of love and mercy that binds up our wounds. If we sunder the cross from the Resurrection, then we tell a tale replicated innumerable times in the human story. Other men and women have been into a darkness that looks like this darkness, and cried with similar pain.

112

If we recount the story of Christ risen from the dead then we proclaim something that is unique and matchless. The cross is not simply a sign of God's emptying of himself into our life and sharing our dreadful predicaments, it is a sign that we are drawn into his life through the Resurrection. As the fathers of the early church expressed it, 'He became as we are that we might become as he is'.

Yet, pain can hold a dark fascination for Christians. For some it has been seen as desirable, a way of achieving union with God. Others, wracked with guilt, have seen pain as a means of repaying the debt of their sins. Christianity has, at times, been haunted by sado-masochism, the need to punish, to inflict pain, or to suffer and glory in pain. There is a lingering belief that pain in itself is a way of dealing with the world and improving its condition. Our theologies are geared far more to pain than they are to happiness. We know, or so we believe, the purposes that pain fulfils and the lessons it teaches us. It is God's favourite lecture room where he communicates the inner secrets of the faith. We are not nearly so convinced that happiness serves any higher purpose than that of guilding the present moment. A theology of happiness is hard-pressed to find words and meanings that will lift the experience of it into the everlasting purposes of God.

On his way as a prisoner to Rome, the first-century bishop Ignatius of Antioch, wrote ahead to the church there and pleaded with them to take no steps that would deliver him from the martyrdom upon which he had set his heart. 'I am writing to all the churches and I enjoin all, that I am dying willingly for God's sake, if only you do not prevent it. I beg of you, do not do me an untimely kindness. Allow me to be eaten by the beasts, which are my way of reaching to God. I am God's wheat, and I am to be ground by the teeth of wild beasts, so that I may become the pure bread of Christ.'[1]. Centuries later, Thérèse of Lisieux longed for martyrdom and made an act of oblation to God in which she prayed, 'I offer myself as a

sacrificial victim to your merciful love, asking you to con-
sume me incessantly, allowing the waves of infinite tender-
ness within you to overflow into my soul, and that thus I
may become a martyr of your love, O my God'. A year
later, the first symptoms of the tuberculosis that was to
take her life seventeen months later made their appearance.
This was to be her martyrdom, a lingering death, subjected
to painful medical treatment and without resort to pain
killers which her Mother Superior did not offer and for
which Thérèse refused to ask.

We are here in a strange milieu. On the one hand, it
displays an almost perverse, yet moving, courage and, on
the other, it seems to betray a longing for the destruction
of the body as a means of discovering the self that we might
deplore in others. The Church invariably hails the saints
who seek out pain, who long for it and strap it to their
bodies like a cross of nails. Pain, it seems, is God's chosen
instrument of sanctity: pain, not simply accepted, but asked
for.

Yet one of the central concerns of Christian theology is
that of reconciling the existence of pain with our belief in
a good and loving God. The questions we ask are little
different in essence from the questions asked by other
human beings. Why is there suffering? Why this person or
that? Why me? Saints may go looking for ravenous lions
or long to be broken on the wheel, but we feel no attraction
to pain and are hard put to set it within the context of God's
loving purpose. We may admire, yet be utterly baffled by,
Thérèse's oblation of herself as a martyr. In the moments
of darkness and doubt during her last illness, however, she
explores a terrain more familiar to us and one which draws
us closer to her.

God is able to bring great glory out of suffering. There
may even be times when we have to elect to suffer, or to
accept pain as the means of achieving some greater goal.
What is doubtful is that we should be enamoured with
pain or, worst of all, in some unconscious way, long for it

as a means of being punished. Our theology addresses the right question – why is there suffering in a world created by a God whose nature is love and mercy? Though God used death as the means to resurrection and renewal, it is his enemy and the last enemy of us all, yet to be destroyed. Similarly with pain. We are not asked to welcome it and embrace it. We are asked to believe that it is a dark night during which we may more clearly see God's light and a means of more deeply entering into union with Christ crucified and risen. The reason for this lies not in any virtue of the pain itself, (it has none), but in the grace of God that is sovereign even where pain seems to hold sway.

There are features of pain that increase the intensity of its hold over us.

The first is loneliness. Pain is deeply personal, it is ours and there is no way in which it can be transferred to other people. It makes us more aware of our own bodies. Most of the time we are not consciously aware of them. We use our faculties, we send instinctive and unconscious commands to our limbs and take it for granted that our commands will be obeyed. When suffering comes, we discover how lonely it is to be the only occupant of our bodies. There is no one else, deep inside us, going through the same experience of pain as we are. The load cannot be distributed.

Our sense of loneliness is sharpened by the difficulty we experience in communicating what we feel to others. We may be surrounded by sympathetic and loving people, but they are outside of us, not inside where the pain is. We may try to communicate what we feel, to put it all into words. Our success in doing so, however, does not rest with our eloquence but with the skills of the listener and his or her willingness to empathise.

Pain isolates us. Sometimes it does this physically by taking us out of our customary environment or interrupting our usual routine. We may find ourselves unable to carry out our normal duties. An illness may require hospitalisation. Placed in a strange and sometimes fearful environment, we become aware, when deprived of them, how much our sense of personal identity owes to our usual surroundings. The work we do, the people to whom we relate, our sense of well-being, all contribute to our knowledge of ourselves. We grow accustomed to seeing ourselves against a familiar back-cloth.

In our isolation, we are aware of the world continuing to turn and of people, free of the constraints of pain, able to carry on as normal. There are moments that heighten that sense of isolation. Bereaved, we travel in the funeral cortege, passing people for whom nothing has stopped. Through the car windows we see them, hurrying to their next appointment, standing in conversation with a friend, mothers pushing prams that are carrying little children for whom the world has scarcely begun, shopping, waiting for buses. Our world, so full of pain at our loss, is placed in a world where everything is normal and life has undergone no irreversible change.

In the hospital ward, the visitors come and go, leaving us to the night, our restlessness, our imaginings. Wheeled to the operating theatre, in the daze of pre-medication drugs, we are recumbent and helpless, surrounded by people who are busy and who will not be coming with us into that country beyond the anaesthetising injection.

We discover how little we know of ourselves. Who am I? Fearful of the next wave of pain, relating to a body about to be cut by the surgeon's knife, lying in bed in a strange gown tied at the back, we struggle to detach ourselves from this strange, unrecognisable and isolated figure. To escape from the intolerable loneliness, we try to join the spectators.

Pain also faces us with the theological conundrum at which we have already glanced. We find it hard to reconcile with the God revealed to us in Jesus Christ. The saints who ask for suffering and receive it, at least empty it of one of its most difficult aspects, that of uncertainty. They choose the time and the place of conflict and know what the struggle is all about. For most people, suffering has no respect of time or place, nor is it always seen as a messenger of God. Far from operating as a penal corrective, suffering upsets the scales of justice.

Thousands of children are born whole and healthy, a minority are handicapped from the day of their birth. Natural forces seem to stumble against one another blindly, converge, and bring to birth this child who must be a warrior in the field of suffering. The span of our lives is erratic, unrelated to other people's need of us or of our longings to see things through. Why does this devoted mother die, long, long, before her time? Why do some people die at thirty, cut down and drifting painfully and unwillingly towards their death, yet this person lives to ninety, blessed by friends and family and, finally, taking leave in her sleep?

These are the questions that can make suffering more painful. In an effort to reduce the pain that they bring us, we attempt to impose theories that set out to explain the causes of pain. Some people, comforted by tidiness and logic, however strange, find them helpful. Suffering is a consequence of sin, some say. In the time of Job, there were those who believed that God rewarded the good with prosperity, and visited the wrongdoer with suffering. Where does that leave me? asked the bereaved, impoverished, lonely, suffering Job. Pain is God's way of teaching us lessons, say others, and are comforted by it. Others, Job from the midst of Scripture amongst them, cry out in anger against the capricious nature of suffering. As a malfunction of the natural order, a deep-seated tumour in the brain is explicable; as a form of punishment for sin, it is an outrage and violation of natural justice. As a teaching method, pain belongs to a barbarous past to which we would not now willingly subject our children.

We must, in a moment, come back to the question of theology and Christian responses to pain. At this stage, we must be willing to recognise our solidarity with other men and women and to acknowledge that our bodies are not less vulnerable than theirs and our questions no less fraught and painful. We try to pacify pain by rushing in with our explanations and our theories. We can be too precipitate, by half. We have to begin by accepting our humanity, with its pain, its anger, its bewilderment and what is happening to us. We must not put pain in a bright Christian package that will conceal its cruelty and make it more acceptable to ourselves and others. If we deny our humanity and our sense of outrage and impotence then these will boil beneath the cosmetic veneer with which we cover our suffering.

The third characteristic of pain is that it can engage all our faculties. In childhood, amongst our first experiences of pain is toothache. Our skills are engaged in avoiding variations of heat and cold lest the searing pain run through our jaw. Whatever else we do, however hard we try to concentrate, the pain thuds in our face and demands our entire attention. At night, we move on the pillow, looking for relief, longing for sleep. If we are very young, mercifully we are allowed to cry with the pain.

Some people never experience that degree of physical pain again. Few escape its mental equivalent. Loss, failure, broken relationships, bereavement can all engulf us and colour our perceptions of everything. But, for some, pain is an all too physical reality. Following his heart attack, a friend once described it to me. When it was happening, no thoughts of God or of anything or anyone else ran through his head. There was nothing but the pain, which seemed to fill his whole body and demand all his resources. The pain asked everything of him, without remainder.

To begin with toothache and move to heart attack might seem lacking in a sense of proportion. Such wide parameters do, however, draw us all within the field of pain. We all have some memory of it. It is salutary when we try

to dissect and analyse other people's pain or imagine how
we will cope with our own, should it come. We will know
that, in such moments, we cannot neatly divide ourselves
into bits of mind, soul and body. Suffering will remind us
of what we should need no reminding. We are human. We
are flesh and blood. As Christians we hold only one weapon
in the war against suffering. It is faith.

Sometimes our suffering is caused by being caught up in
the suffering of those we love. It is an experience in which
we learn much about pain and about ourselves.

When we love people very much, we invest our happiness
in theirs, we allow our lives to be drawn into theirs and
theirs into ours. This love is a great privilege and also a
great joy. We may know, somewhere in the back of our
minds, that on some, distant day, suffering will intrude
into our lives and lay its cold touch on what is now alive
and vibrant. We do not dwell on such thoughts. They
lie dormant, largely academic, whilst we live each day,
strengthening the bonds that bind us together, storing up
our memories and dreaming of tomorrow's possibilities.
Sometimes, when we reflect on our happiness, a hint of
fear will snipe at the borders of our mind as we contemplate
its loss. Suffering poses its threat to the treasure that love
has amassed.

If suffering does come to the beloved, we will probably
never forget the way of its coming. Pain makes it first
appearance, the body begins to display the symptoms of
disease, anxiety begins to seep, like bile, into the blood-
stream, doctors are visited, diagnoses are made and con-
firmed. If bad, we know that the enemy has invaded our
territory. Now every memory comes both to comfort and
to mock as we realise the enormity of what we might lose.
Every day is invested with meaning, and all its possibilities
wrung from its hours. Our dreams for the future do not
die, but become more urgent. There is no long passage of

time in which to wait for them leisurely to come true.
Next year must be captured in tomorrow. Nothing must be
allowed to slip through our fingers, tasks left unfinished,
words left unspoken, love left uncelebrated.

We find ourselves isolated in a way that mirrors the
isolation of the sufferer. The suffering of people we love lets
loose fears within us that we are unable to communicate to
others. It numbs us. We also find that we are standing
outside something that we profoundly wish to share; until
now, everything has been shared. We have done so much
together: we have grown together, faced disappointments
and experienced joys together, we have eaten together, we
have prayed together, we have been together in love. There
remains in everyone, a citadel of the self that is never
completely known to anyone else, even those closest to us.
Where there is love, however, that inward, private world
of the self poses no threats, it conceals nothing that we have
to fear. Until suffering comes. Then this inward citadel of
the beloved becomes the scene of a lonely battle in which
we yearn to be an ally. We want to be close to the action
and engage in the hand-to-hand fighting.

There may come a moment in the beloved's suffering
when we want nothing more than to take the pain into our
own bodies. If a husband can recall taking turns with his
wife to sit with a sick child throughout the night, so now
he will wish that it were possible to take turns in bearing
the pain. We fantasise about rotas of pain, each of us awake
to it for four-hour watches, taking our turn whilst the other
sleeps peacefully. It cannot be. We are unable to share the
one thing we long to share. All we can do is make our daily
watchful voyage around this island of pain, always within
hailing distance, always a physical and visible presence to
reassure, always offering the one thing that is ours to offer
– the love we bear.

We are also caught up in the questions that suffering
poses. Often, the questions will be more acute for the one
who witnesses the pain of a loved one than for the one who

suffers. Those who suffer are more hard-pressed to answer the question, 'How am I to bear it?' rather than, 'Why is this happening to me?' It is the one who watches who most feels the anger and the helplessness. A parent will ask, 'Why my child?'; a wife, 'Why my husband?'; and friends, 'Why him? Why her?'

Yet we know that now is not the time to seek explanations. The heart is too overwhelmed by what is happening, the will too engaged in what has to be done for the one who suffers, for the mind to spend its energies in resolving the greatest of all mysteries. Rather, we have to work through the anger and helplessness. The rage has to be channelled into loving commitment to the one who suffers and the helplessness refuse to be mesmerised into inactivity by what is happening.

Just as suffering invades all our faculties, so to be the witness of suffering requires a complete giving of ourselves to the other. The suffering of someone we love involves us in a *kenosis*, an emptying of ourselves. Just as the sufferer's pain may absorb all of his or her faculties, so sharing the experience of someone we love requires that same degree of absorbtion. Our abhorrence at the physical pain and what it does to people who have been to us signs of joy and vitality, any pity that we may feel for our own predicament, our fears for the future, all of these are transcended by the need to be love to the one whom we love.

Thérèse's Little Way takes on a poignant meaning. All our energies are directed to the next moment, the next thing that has to be done, the next word to be spoken, the next silence to be vigilantly shared. In a strange way, the one who suffers and the one who watches become Christ to each other. For the sufferer, to be 'crucified with Christ' takes on a meaning that could not have been visualised in the moment of her baptism in water. The pain has become that other baptism of which Christ spoke, the baptism in blood. So the sufferer, united with Christ in her pain, becomes a sign of Christ crucified. She suffers in him, and he in her. We may not agree that some of the saints were right to ask for pain, but we begin to form some notion of what they were after. Pain is a union with Christ crucified, a moment of intense and total identification with him. To watch with someone who suffers is to stand with the women at the foot of the cross and to see God descending into the darkest places of the earth.

By God's grace, the one who watches is also Christ to the one who suffers. The words of reassurance and comfort are Christ's words; the hand fondly held rests in the palm of his hand; the loving presence is his presence. Christ touches our humanity, in our suffering and in our watching. He enters into both and each ministers to the other in his and her starkly different ways. In Christ, we are united and Christ holds us both.

There may come a time when the suffering is ours and others watch with us as we make our journey through the valley of the shadow. None of us can say how we will react when and if that time comes. We may draw comfort from the fact that most people underestimate their reserves of courage and resilience. What we do know, if we have shared the suffering of someone else, is that the landscape of our own suffering will not be wholly unfamiliar. Our isolation will be less hard to bear in the knowledge that someone we loved came this way before us.

Away from the field of suffering, we can ask ourselves how pain relates to the God whom we have tried to describe so far. What place does suffering have in our belief in a God who invests us with freedom, who himself lives in freedom and openness to the future, who does not coerce us nor manipulate events around us, who calls us into partnership with himself and invites us on a journey of faith?

When it comes to suffering, some people may find it hard to go on believing in that sort of God. One of the harsh things about suffering is its arbitrary nature. Pain seems to run amok amongst human beings, insensitive to where it strikes. As I write this, imprinted on my mind is a photograph of an eighteen-year-old German girl on the front page of this morning's newspaper. She is being held by a young criminal who, with two companions, crazed by a mixture of alcohol and drugs, unsuccessfully tried to rob a bank. In their escape, they took the girl as a hostage. In the photograph she looks out with frightened eyes from the back of a car, as the robber holds his pistol to her throat. It was the last picture of a girl at the threshold of her life. This morning, she is dead, shot by her captor who is now in police hands.

She was in the wrong place at the wrong time. One insignificant decision might have taken her by another route, or found her somewhere else in the moment of danger. A year before she might have chosen another job in another part of the city. Before her birth, her parents might have chosen to live in another place. The possibilities send us reeling back into the hours and decades before this fateful moment.

Because pain is so arbitrary, some people need to turn to a God who controls everything. They need to believe that, whatever happens, his will is being done. Better, they feel, a God who is in charge than that pain should strike in this haphazard way.

Whatever the comfort derived by them from this belief, there are two flaws in it. The first is that God is made the author of pain, either because he wills it or permits it. As a conceptual abstraction, such a thought may be bearable. But in the midst of suffering it becomes counterproductive. As we watch someone we love in great pain, as disease drains life from his or her body, the thought that God wills this to happen or that he permits it to happen rather than intervene, becomes intolerable. The second problem is that the belief that God wills all things places us back in a determinist cosmos. The degree of cellular and congenital control required to bring about the appearance of a cancer in a particular person's body at a particular time is quite incompatible with any real belief in freedom.

In his book *When Bad Things Happen to Good People*, Rabbi Harold Kushner thought through the issues of suffering as he came to terms with the death of his fourteen-year-old son from progeria or 'rapid ageing'. He saw tragedies of this sort as a consequence, not of God's choice or will, but of living in a world which is not yet fully ordered and living in perfect harmony. There remain pockets of chaos, or randomness. Suffering events 'happen at random, and randomness is another name for chaos, in those corners of the universe where God's creative light has not yet penetrated. And chaos is evil; not wrong, not malevolent, but evil nonetheless, because by causing tragedies at random, it prevents people from believing in God's goodness'.[2]

God invests all things with freedom and, with infinite patience, draws them into partnership with himself. His work is one of drawing together and reconciling everything in the universe that is at odds with its surroundings, that finds itself in natural conflict and a struggle for survival. Nothing possesses absolute freedom. Every living component operates within the freedom of its own kind. It lives and acts according to its own nature. A great deal of the created order does not have the power of decision. A tornado cannot decide to blow east instead of west, nor malignant cells decide to attack healthy cells. Chaos is never complete, since all things live within the nature of their own being. Even our freedom as human beings is circumscribed by who we are and where we are.

This complex interaction of the innumerable components of the created order, with the occasional randomness that finds its way into human experience in the form of suffering, does not leave us with an indifferent God. We are not talking of the watchmaker God, beloved of eighteenth-century deists, winding up the universe and passively watching it run down. It would be absurd to deny to the creator the freedom with which he has invested his creatures, or to ascribe him a role apart from the dynamic interaction of the created order. He, too, exercises his freedom within the world, acting in conformity with his own nature of love and justice. He does so, not by manipulation of his creatures, but by working with them and through them.

Where Christ's Lordship is acknowledged, the Holy Spirit influences, encourages and inspires men and women in their actions. It is out of their response, in their willingness to find their perfect freedom by being the agents of his will, that God is able to move with all things towards the coming fulfilment of his purposes. His will is also retroactive, however. Where there is chaos and pain; where suffering results, not from his decision to make it happen but from the disordered interaction of independent and unreconciled agents, he is free to gather up and incorporate that suffering into his will.

This does not mean that all suffering is given a happy ending, all problems provided a solution, all evil emptied of its power. There can be no happy ending to the story of the Jewish Holocaust. The suffering of our loved ones is in no way diminished by the consequences that follow from their pain. God present and active in his freedom is able, however, to strengthen our will to survive, to give us the grace to channel our grief and loss into a love that will keep us from the corrosion of bitterness, to bring hope out of despair. His will is seen to be done not in inflicting pain upon those who suffer but in the legacy they leave in the hearts and minds of those who have been the witnesses of their suffering. We may not be free to choose whether we or our loved ones will suffer, we are free to choose what that suffering will make of our humanity. We are free to twist the Devil's nose and to turn some of the fiercest weapons in the armoury of evil into a way of making the world a place in which God is glorified and our humanity enhanced.

The God who is with us in suffering is the God who is made known to us supremely in Jesus Christ, crucified and risen from the dead. Our understanding of suffering and the nature of God's presence will be shaped by our belief in the cross and resurrection. For the cross is God's way of totally identifying himself with us in our suffering. Here, in Christ, he stands in solidarity with us and descends into the depths of our pain. At the cross, there is nothing to which Christ remains a stranger, either physical pain, or rejection, or darkness, or a sense of the divine absence, or death itself. It is the dark and fearful path by which he comes to the glory of his resurrection. In his journey through the darkness into the light, through death into life, he takes us in solidarity with him, bringing us through our own suffering into the glory of his risen life. When Jesus was raised from the dead, he brought our humanity with him, a humanity now made glorious, imperishable and incorruptible.

The cross and the Resurrection are our way to understanding and enduring our suffering. Yet it is a way always seen and lived in faith. It is not a template that we can place over all pain, believing that here and now, all suffering will end and a new life begin. Our belief in the cross and the Resurrection has to straddle this life and the life to come, it has to hold in faith what is seen now and what is yet to be seen.

Christ crucified and risen is present in our darkness, always to heal and bless. There will be times when his presence, and the grace which he releases into a situation, will interact with the forces that have converged to bring about the pain. There is an area of mystery in disease and pain that lies beyond the scope of medical and scientific knowledge, depths where the dynamic interplay of physical, emotional and spiritual factors will result in the regression of disease and deliverance from pain. Healing will be seen as the sufferer emerges from her darkness into a new life that resembles nothing so much as it resembles resurrection.

At other times, his healing presence will contain the disruptive powers of pain. Jesus told us that we should fear him who can destroy the soul more than we fear the destruction of the body. Pain can attack our inner integrity, it can sow its seeds of bitterness and fear in our hearts, it can take away our peace and undermine our faith. The inner, healing presence of Christ transfigures suffering, bringing from it a very different harvest. Those who have suffered and those who have watched know that Christ has been the most powerful factor within their ordeal. His presence has been a profound and mysterious reality within which they have lived through the experience. As the sufferer engages all her faculties to cope with pain, as the watcher gathers all his to empty himself into the other's need, Christ has held both within his hands. He has replenished the sources of grace, his Spirit has prayed the prayers for which our lips could find no words, the light of his resurrection has shimmered like a halo of light around the darkness we have shared.

The 'hidden God', we find, is concealed within our pain as surely as he was concealed within the sufferings of Christ upon the cross. Side by side with our anger at what suffering has done, and the memory of the ordeal through which people we love may have lived, there is the testimony that we can never deny – that Christ was there and somehow the night became as the day and our emptiness a way of knowing. Pain strips us until we are left with nothing save 'naked faith'. When all the trappings and embellishments with which we dress up our humanity are taken away, when pain itself has disfigured and distorted the body that is our home, yet there is left that humanity which, day by day, increasingly reflects the image of God.

The last healing of all is the healing of our death. It is here, in faith and in hope, that we affirm the risen life of Christ and our risen life in him and through him. If we judge the 'success' of our prayers and our hopes of healing simply by the reversal of disease and our restoration to health in this life, then we limit the sovereignty of Christ's risen life. To die is not to fail. To witness the death of someone we love is not to have failed in our praying, or in our loving, or in our faith. Death is the final completion of this earthly chapter. It is the final binding of our wounds in utterly healing love. It is the fulfilment of our humanity in that new humanity which is in Christ and which, springing from this world, finds its completion in the world to come.

At last, we shall be free. Perhaps only then shall we fully understand the ways of suffering. Until then, we grasp the carefree days of our joys with eager and grateful hands. And, when suffering comes, we believe that Christ will be with us.

Notes

1 Ignatius of Antioch *Letter to the Romans* 4.1.
2 Kushner, Harold *When Bad Things Happen to Good People* (London: Pan 1982) p.61.

Chapter Eight

The Goal of our Journey

In the best of journeys, the end provides a climax to all that has gone before. There is a gathering of strength and momentum that pushes us towards the goal that we had set ourselves. We arrive at what we discover to be the best of all times and the most desirable of all places. We stand on a height from which we can look back and trace the way we came. We shake off the fatigue of our journey and find our resources renewed by the sheer sense of achievement.

The human journey is not always like that. There are people for whom the latter part of their journey is the crowning glory to all that has gone before. They are in possession of all their faculties. Their opinion is sought. Their company is still valued by those who love them. They arrive at their death in quietness and peace and are remembered with great gratitude by those who survive them.

For many, it is different. The peak of our mental and physical powers is reached before the last stretch of the journey. That is a truth that we would recognise and find little difficulty in accepting. What is harder to accept is the decline of our spiritual strength. We cannot deny the interdependence of all our faculties. When the mind and body begin to fade, the spirit begins to fade with them.

It is a time when, much of our energy spent and our faculties no longer responding as once they did, there is

129

required of us one long, last bursting commitment to all that we have believed in and trusted. Like an athlete at the end of a long-distance run, reaching the last lap, we have to summon up strength, we know not how, from our shattered and scattered resources.

The great French Jesuit and scientist, Teilhard de Chardin, looked to the coming of that part of his life.

When the erosions of age begin to leave their mark on my body, and still more on my mind; when the ills that must diminish my life or put an end to it strike me down from without or grow up from within me; when I reach that painful moment when I suddenly realise that I am a sick man or that I am growing old; above all at that final moment when I feel that I am losing hold on myself and becoming wholly passive in the hands of those great unknown forces which first formed me: at all these sombre moments grant me, Lord, to understand that it is you (provided my faith is strong enough) who are painfully separating the fibres of my being so as to penetrate to the very marrow of my substance and draw me to yourself.[1]

Teilhard's words are full of insight. He recognises that the changes in our body and mind are beyond our control. As Canute demonstrated to his foolish courtiers, there is no human word that can push back the inevitable, whether it be the flow of the tide or the ageing of our bodies or the coming of disease. Yet if age and sickness have their part in what is happening to us, so does Christ. By the consent of our faith, he begins the work of sundering our enduring self from the body which has been its faithful servant. Just as our mothers, when we were very small, helped us to undress at night, to take off our clothes at the end of the day, so Christ begins to divest us of our ageing and ailing bodies. At the end of our lives, he is mother to us, preparing us for the final rest that will lead to tomorrow's endless day.

It is Christ who has been our companion throughout. It is through him that we have known as much as it is possible for us to know of God. In him, we discovered humanity, our own and that of other people, and learned to love and value it. Jesus is the Way, the Truth and the Life. He is the journey; he is the truth towards which we travel and by which we live; and he is the life that is in our life, as ours is the life that is in his.

We have rigorously kept the cross at the centre of our vision of Christ. In the cross, we see the totality of Christ's solidarity with us in our humanity; we see the nature of God and understand his ways of working with us; and we are able to interpret our human experiences and realise the presence of Christ within them.

The cross, however, can be all these things to us only through the Resurrection. The Resurrection is not a spiritual postscript to Christ's incarnation, a return to his pre-existent being. It is the destination of our human journey. Christ brings us with him from the other side of the tomb, and what he is there, we are to become. The Resurrection is central, not only to the doctrine of salvation, but also to that of creation. It does not simply tell us how we are saved, nor is it limited to providing a hope for believing Christians. It is a harbinger of the destiny of all things. The Resurrection of Christ is the guarantee of the final restitution of the entire created order. The story, begun in the primeval chaos from which, in the succession of aeon upon aeon, God eventually brought our humanity, fashioned, male and female, in his own image, finds its destiny in that Christ who appeared to Mary Magdalen on the morning of the Resurrection. The nature and veracity of the Resurrection are of central importance, not simply because a certain theory of scriptural authority may be at stake, or because it is a central tenent of the Church's historic tradition, but because only in it can we know where our humanity is bound for. Just as it is pivotal to the integrity of the Christian faith, so it is essential to our understanding of what it means to be human.

If we are to interpret the significance of the Resurrection for our journey in Christ, then we have to hold three things together: the Gospel accounts of the Resurrection, Paul's profound teaching on the nature of resurrection as given in 1 Corinthians 15, and the ascension of our Lord.

For an event of such fundamental importance to the stories of creation and salvation, the Resurrection is an event that takes place with very little drama. Christ appears to those who love him and have believed in him. He does not come to demonstrate to the Sanhedrin the dreadful miscarriage of their justice, nor to Pilate the errors of his judgement. He does not appear to the crowds still gathered in Jerusalem for Passover, nor retrace the Via Dolorosa that all might see that he who was dead is alive again. He comes to the few who knew him most intimately.

These to whom he comes, either do not recognise him or are initially frightened at his coming. Mary failed to recognise him, the travellers to Emmaus likewise, as also the disciples returning from their night of futile fishing and seeing him standing on the beach.[2] This failure to recognise can be interpreted either as a blindness brought on by grief, or by a divine intervention, an intentional scaling of human eyes by God, or because a change had taken place in Christ himself. It is this latter that points us to a theology of resurrection. What the disciples saw was our Lord and yet, in some mysterious way, he had been transfigured. There were the signs of his identity, even the marks of the nails, and yet his body had undergone a transfiguration. This was Jesus, raised from the dead, but not simply restored to his former life. Jesus was not like Lazarus. Indeed, the raising of Lazarus raises problems that the Resurrection of Jesus does not. Lazarus would grow old and one day he would die again. We know that Christ, having once died, will never die again. Nor will the body of the resurrection be subject to fresh pains, nor decay through the process of ageing.

The realisation that Jesus has moved on to another order, or reality, which has no precedence in our human story, is captured in the story of the encounter between Mary Magdalen and Jesus in the garden.[3] Jesus uses those strange words. 'Do not cling to me'. Our imaginations can picture what John has not fully described. In the moment of recognition, Magdalen embraced Jesus, held him with the passion and gratitude of someone who had seen the world taken away from her and who now believed that, marvellously and joyously, it had been given back to her. Yet that is precisely how the event of the Resurrection was not to be understood. The world as it was had not been given back to her. Jesus had not been raised in order that everything might be left unchanged and returned to what it had been before his death on the cross. The reason for our Lord's apparent rejection of Magdalen's embraces is made clear in the words that follow: 'I have not yet ascended to the Father. But go to my brothers, and tell them that I am now ascending to my Father and your Father, to my God and your God'. Jesus is still talking of journeying. Mary wants to cling to the present or, if journeys are to be made, to retrace her steps to the past. Jesus directs her to a future which lies in God's fullness and which is to be shared by all his people. It is a future that does not diminish or exclude the love with which she embraces him, but one in which that love is caught up in the vast love of God. It is a future in which those we love will never again be crucified and those who share it will never again have to look back to the past for their happiness. As long as Mary clung to Jesus, believing that the past had been restored to her, she could make no headway in that journey towards a more glorious future.

The nature of the destiny, which we come to through

the resurrection of our Lord, is central to Paul's treatment of the resurrection body in 1 Corinthians 15. He, too, recounts the Gospel accounts of the appearances of Jesus as evidence of the Resurrection. But he goes beyond the simple historical accounts to wrestle with the nature and meaning of resurrection. 'Flesh and blood can never possess the kingdom of God, and the perishable cannot possess immortality', he tells us.

Whatever else it was that the disciples witnessed in the Resurrection of our Lord, it was not the resuscitation without change of the body which had been laid to rest in the tomb. Paul's discussion of the Resurrection arises naturally from his account of the Church's testimony to the Risen Christ. The Resurrection that we are all to share and which, one day, will gather up all creation, is the resurrection that has already been witnessed in the raising of Jesus Christ from the dead. Faith believes that what Christ has become we are to become. His earthly body was, and ours shall be, a body sown in the earth, a perishable reality and raised imperishable; it had been laid down in its humiliating destruction by man's violence and raised in glory; it had succumbed to death in its weakness and been raised in power; it had been laid in the tomb an 'animal body', a body of this earth, belonging to and part of it, but raised a spiritual body and caught up in God's glory. And because it was caught up in that glory, we shall all share it when all the enemies of our humanity have been put down, the last enemy to be destroyed being death itself.

It is this glorified body that Christ took with him into the triune life of God. The Ascension is the Church's testimony that humanity has been received into the Godhead. The eternal fellowship of the Father, Son and Holy Spirit, that active, moving love from which all things derive their life and being, has now received into itself, in Christ, our humanity. It is this, incredibly, of which our Lord spoke when he said, 'I go to prepare a place for you'.[4] The purpose to which God has held from the creation of man and woman in his own image to this very latest moment in the story of creation is that, at last, we might share his life, he receiving to himself our humanity and we being transfigured by his divinity. From Bethlehem to Olivet the sacred mystery comes full circle, 'He became as we are, that we might become as he is'.

It is this glorified body and blood of Jesus Christ that we receive at the Holy Table. For there, again as Paul tells us, we have fellowship with his body and blood.[5] The presence of Christ in the Eucharist is substantial and real, not because it restores to us, here and now, the incarnate Christ in his earthly vulnerability, but because it gives to us a reality fashioned out of the stuff of glory. Even now, through sacramental grace, we taste of that life which is to come and are given a share of that glory which is one day to be ours. The heavenly food that does not fail is the glorified body and blood of the Risen and Ascended Lord.

Between this life and our final transfiguration in Christ lies our death. It is easy for none of us to speak of our death. We do not know the time or the manner of its coming. Thérèse of Lisieux, her ardent heart full of images of her Normandy heroine Joan of Arc, dreamt of martyrdom. She longed for a death that was a loving self-immolation, a gesture of courage and a witness to what she believed in. When death came, it came early yet dragged its feet. Not for her the final brief moments engulfed in flames and agonising pain, but months in which disease, slowly and with cruel refinement, ate away at her lungs. Similarly, as bravely as we might anticipate our end, we do not choose either the time or the place.

Yet, surrounded as death is by uncertainty and by our natural fears, we should not succumb to the modern tendency to conceal its existence. The prayers of the Christian tradition have accustomed the men and women who have prayed them to living with the thought of their own death.

For centuries, people have prayed that God might fill every part of them, head, understanding, mouth, heart and –

God be at mine end, and at my departing.

In the Ave Maria, Catholics have prayed that Mary would 'pray for us sinners now, and at the hour of our death'. Countless congregations, at the end of the day, have sung Thomas Ken's words –

> Teach me to live, that I may dread
> The grave as little as my bed;
> Teach me to die, that so I may
> Rise glorious at the judgement day.

These have not been prayers reserved for special times of adversity or of trauma. They have formed part of the daily pattern of prayer from childhood to old age. They have reminded those who prayed them that this life ends in our death. They have enabled people to grow familiar with their own mortality.

Amongst evangelicals in the eighteenth century, young children were taken to a death bed in order that they might see how a Christian dies. This was done in no morbid, oppressive spirit. In times when infant mortality was high and every family experienced the death of a child, when people died at home rather than behind the bedside screens in a hospital ward, death was no stranger. It was believed that Christians, from an early age, might grow not fearing death, believing that Christ through his resurrection had overcome its power.

In the twentieth century, we see more people die than did these forebears. We are saturated with violence. We see death from war, terrorism and starvation on the television screen. Television drama portrays people shot down, accompanied by the quiet thud of the silenced gun, or flailing dramatically as their bodies are raked by machine gun fire. But it is all at a number of removes from us. We see it through glazed eyes. We have to remind ourselves that it is real. It does not prepare us for the look, the touch, the smell of someone whom we love dying before our eyes, nor for the fateful realisation, one day, that we are dying ourselves.

The Christian faith both reminds us that all those people of whose deaths we are distant and mechanical witnesses, are men and women with a story and no less subject to pain and fear than are we, and that we ourselves must die. It does this whilst affirming this life, calling us to our duties within God's creation, and encouraging us to celebrate our humanity. It does not face men and women with false alternatives of loving this world and seeking justice on this earth, or preparing for death and keeping clear the vision of the City of God which lies in the world which is to come. We are called to live out our humanity here, and to trust in the final transfiguration of our humanity through our death and in the life to come.

We prepare for our death every time we 'let go', beginning with our birth when we have to let go of our mother's womb. Every time we say farewell, every stage of our lives we leave behind, through childhood, youth, young adulthood, early and late middle age, every occasion we have to pull up roots and move on, every loss of what seemed permanent and secure, is a preparation for our last farewell, the penultimate stage of the journey, the last painful wresting of our roots from the world that has been our home, the final destruction of every support and security, leaving us with nothing save faith. In different ways, we spend our lives dying and, in the midst of life, being born again.

Yet, in Christ, we unashamedly confess our faith in that City towards which we travel. We are caught up in the vision of seers and prophets who so touchingly glimpsed the mingling of the human with divine glory. Like Isaiah, who saw the predator and the hunted lying together without the desire to kill or the need to run away, rejoiced at the sight of a child dancing, unharmed, on the viper's nest, and saw all gathered to a holy mountain where none would hurt or destroy.[6] Like Zechariah, who saw the streets of a city in which old men sat and talked together in the light of the midday sun, and heard the echoing sound of children's laughter.[7] Like John, who saw Jerusalem which he knew and loved, descending from heaven, God standing in her midst where the Temple had once stood, his glorious and tranquil light filling the whole place.[8]

Always the dreams are the same. The familiar, the loved, the truly human is taken up and transfigured, gathered into the everlasting bliss of the triune God.

It will be so for us. The lame will limp no more, and the disabled will climb to the summit of God's mountain. The blind will open their eyes in astonishment. The broken will be made whole and the wounded healed. Love will make us one, and never again will we be sundered apart. We will find a happiness that no longer needs the dark shadows of pain to give it brightness. Nor will it be taken from us lest we grow selfish and forgetful, for it will be written on our hearts that God is love and all things are held in his grace. None will be enslaved nor any man or woman hold others to be their inferiors. We will dance in the streets of the city and, on the hillsides, we will recount to one another God's goodness to us. We will tell the stories of creation and recall with wonder the cross. We will make music.

At last, we shall have arrived at our home. Yet, who knows what other journeys may await us within the limitless possibilities of God's eternity?

Notes

1   Teilhard de Chardin *Hymn of the Universe* (London: Collins 1965) p. 104.
2   John 20.14; Luke 24.16; John 21.4.
3   John 20.10–18.

4   John 14.2.
5   1 Corinthians 10.16,17.
6   Isaiah 11.6–9.
7   Zechariah 8.4–5.
8   Revelation 22.5.